Moore to Food

Moore to Food

MICHAEL MOORE

For Eloise and Charlie

CONTENTS

Welcome	8
Thoughts on entertaining	18
Brunch	22
Canapés	52
Entrées	82
Tapas	104
Mains	116
Sides	164
Desserts	180
Cheese	210
Petits Fours	222
Cocktails	236
Basics	252
Glossary	266
Acknowledgments	268
Index of recipes	270

WELCOME

We all know that good food is the main component to any great meal. My study and many years of hands-on experience has taught me that there is *Moore to Food*. There are other key elements in finding the elusive 'x factor' that differentiates the memorable from the ordinary.

At home, comfort is the most important consideration for a great meal. Get the lighting, the music and the company right, mix that with great food and good wine and you may find that special 'moment in time' that defines truly great food. Every day I wake up and go in pursuit of those special moments.

All of the dishes in this book have been created to inspire you to cook and think about food. Each dish has a strong design focus, integrity of raw product and season, a range of textures and colour. They are dynamic and should firstly delight the eye and then excite the tastebuds.

How it all began

The home address on my birth certificate says 'a caravan'. It's true! While our beginnings were humble, our life was rich in food, cooking and laughter. I remember a very happy childhood.

Mum was a natural cook, always making her own bread and biscuits. She would organise great dinner parties and I'd help in the kitchen. My reward was the piece of steak Mum would save on her plate, what a treat!

My sister Lisa and I wished we had the money to buy the 'good stuff' everyone else had at their house; 'boil in the bag' fish and frozen hamburgers (the very thought of it!).

"My grandmothers were both accomplished cooks and a huge influence in my life."

It was only as I grew older that I realised that cooking from scratch with fresh ingredients was far better and more nutritious. I finally understood what mum was about.

From an early age I knew I was going to be a chef, it just all came naturally. At six years old I baked my own birthday cake; a feat I had always been proud of, until now when I watch my beautiful ten-year-old daughter create amazing food without help. My grandmothers were both accomplished cooks and a huge influence in my life. Nanny Moore and I would pick ripe fruit from the roadside in the summer. We'd sterilise jars, make jams and pickles, bake cakes and scones. Nan Jepson made the most amazing Welsh Tea Loaf that took two weeks to complete, and chocolate dipped Florentines wrapped in tissue paper. She was the posh one!

My dad loved the food I cooked and he took it to work to give to his mates; that was a real buzz for me. He did worry about the time I spent in the kitchen. He'd rather I learn real life skills such as painting and putting shelves up like 'proper men do'. Thankfully he has changed his opinion since then.

I had a quick mind and a challenging curiosity. Food was the centre of my universe. I was convinced food was the passport to my dreams and would open the doors to a great life travelling the world.

I could already see distinct advantages. At high school I was the only boy in the home economics class which was great for meeting girls! Year after year I'd win first prize in all the cooking and baking competitions. I never doubted which career path I would choose. I left school with my highest qualifications in cookery and drama (go figure!).

Mum and I went for an interview at one of England's top catering colleges. I was wearing borrowed shoes and jeans and all I could think of was how to get in this course. It was the first time I felt pressure in my life. When I was accepted, I ran up the street jumping for joy! It made my mum so happy and signified the start of a whole new exciting future for me.

I spent three intense years at college studying the principles of classical cookery and food science. Graduating with a High Distinction, I packed my bags and headed for London.

It was the early 1980s and London was a vibrant and exciting place for a young chef. Nouvelle cuisine was in full swing. I started out in some of London's best, including the Café Royal and 45 Park Lane. This was pre Marco Pierre White and Gordon Ramsay.

In those days being a chef was a slog and kitchen life was pretty grim. You needed to be passionate and tough to survive. I worked with some of London's best chefs. They weren't nice people, but I respected them. I was young and arrogant and a bit of a dreamer and desperate to travel. I could cook like the wind and was being influenced by real professionals who were totally committed.

I also worked with young chefs from Australia and was struck by their unique and relaxed

approach to cooking. It was a huge risk for any ambitious chef to turn their back on the kitchens of Europe. After all, this was the epicentre of food. I now faced one of the biggest decisions of my career. Either I was to cultivate my experience in 'classical cuisine' and head to Paris, stay put in London or go on a working holiday and explore 'new world cuisine'. I had wanderlust and had never been on a plane before. The images I had grown up with of sun and sand were too much of a drawcard.

I was living in a house with two chefs and a waiter and we all decided to leave the UK at once. We wrote letters applying for jobs all over the world. About 90 were posted altogether. Waiting for the mail in the coming weeks was exciting. I had an offer from Sydney, the others had offers in Bermuda and New York. We had a massive farewell party and filled the bay windows of our flat with empty beer cans and went our separate ways.

This was a massive turning point in my life. It was my first time on a plane and I was bound for Sydney on a one-year working holiday. I was 21 years old with £400 in my pocket and a loose job offer.

"This was one of the most focused and dynamic kitchens I'd ever worked in and played a significant part in my development as a chef."

I arrived in Sydney and a whole new world opened up to me. I got a job at Kables, a three-hatted restaurant in what used to be the Regent Hotel (now The Four Seasons). I worked with a team of really talented chefs who had a progressive approach to modern cooking.

After a year at Kables, I left Sydney and travelled through Asia, investigating that amazing cuisine. I returned to London to work as the head fish chef at The Ritz Hotel; back to classic cooking with a head full of the new world. The Executive Chef would get me to cook dishes for the food media to demonstrate how progressive his kitchen was. I made some great friends in this kitchen, it was the hardest physical work of my life. We served royalty and celebrities, politicians and prime ministers on a daily basis.

It was here that I had a 'brief encounter' with a gorgeous young female chef. I can tell you this much. The young chef was called Angela and I ended up marrying her seven years later and we've been together 23 years! Her career as a chef lasted six weeks!

By mid-1988, I was back in Sydney. I secured my first Head Chef position at Craigend, a twohatted restaurant and one of Sydney's best at the time. I was 23 years old, ready to work hard and hungry for more. I soon cultivated a media profile, with regular TV appearances and my own radio gig on 2UE.

I met and became good friends with the foodies, top chefs and suppliers of this time.

Sydney had become one of the hottest places in the world to cook in. It was an amazing time. I remember when some top chefs from Europe came to visit and they didn't know what lemongrass was. John Susman, who owned the Flying Squid Brothers, walked into my kitchen one day in a polo shirt and white wellies with a box of Coffin Bay scallops. We've been good mates ever since. John remains one of the leading seafood experts in the country.

Barry MacDonald had a cheese supply business with Simon Johnson called McDonald and Johnson. They supplied King Island cheese and creams, which were considered top quality and hard to come by. Even though now King Island is stocked in every supermarket, to me the Black Label Brie is still one of Australia's finest cheeses. Barry now owns Fratelli Fresh and Simon continued and developed into Simon Johnson Providores. These guys were and still are key influences on the way we eat in Australia.

The hot chefs were Steve Manfredi, Damien Pignolet, Christine Manfield, David Thompson, Paul Merrony, Mark Armstrong and Andrew Blake, who I played golf with every Monday. Andrew ran Chez Oz and was the coolest chef in town. He was probably one of the first 'celebrity chefs' in Australia, appearing in magazines like *Gourmet Traveller* and *Vogue Entertaining*.

Leo Schofield was the big man in the industry as head food reviewer for *The Sydney Morning Herald* and Editor of the *Good Food Guide,* which was only about two years old at the time. He did actually know a lot about style, food and restaurants. I personally believe he made a massive contribution to the development of Australian cuisine.

It was now 1990 and Australia was riding high in the global food scene. With an abundance of fresh local produce, Pacific-Asian influences and the emergence of talented chefs, it was the coming of age of Australian cuisine. Sydney was the most exciting place in the world to be for young and creative chefs.

I had always thrived on leadership and motivation and was taking my chances applying for big jobs. I also fancied myself as a restaurateur, so I started looking at lease opportunities. One day it all landed on my lap. I got a phone call offering me the lease on the bistro at the Windsor Castle Pub. Don't ask me how I was going to pay for it, I was absolutely flat broke. Believe it or not, an hour later I received another call offering me the role of Executive Chef at the Hotel Nikko Darling

Harbour. So in true Michael Moore style, I took on the challenge of both!

I set up the bistro and brought in a partner to run it. I then set my mind to the biggest challenge of my career. I had every confidence I could do something this big. The Nikko was the largest five-star hotel in Australia and at just 26 years old, I was the youngest hotel Executive Chef.

The Corn Exchange Brasserie was highly regarded and featured in *The Sydney Morning Herald Good Food Guide*. In four and a half years, this job really developed me as a leader, mentor and equipped me with the skills to run large-scale operations. I was hungry for more.

In 1995, while on a trip to the UK to get married, I had lunch at Quaglinos in London. I met Head Chef Martin Webb, who later introduced me to Sir Terence Conran, design visionary and founder of one of Britain's most dynamic and successful restaurant groups.

Terence instantly recognised my passion and dynamism and offered me the job of Executive Chef for one of his largest projects, The Bluebird 'Gastrodome' in London's Chelsea. This was a dream. Angela and I jumped at this opportunity and headed back to London. It was the seven-year itch.

With responsibility for a restaurant, private club, food store, production kitchen and café and a team of 120 chefs, I faced my biggest challenge to date. I was involved in all aspects of development, from ground-up design and build through to the operation of this £15 million project. In the course of the pre-opening year, I travelled around the UK and Europe, selecting my kitchen team as well as testing and tasting the entire range of Bluebird's 25,000 products for The Food Store.

Bluebird's high profile attracted the who's who of London's elite, and its critical success resulted in my emergence as one of London's top chefs. This also resulted in radio and television appearances, master classes and cooking workshops around the country including the *BBC Good Food Show*. Terence valued my skills, not only as a chef, but as a leader and operator. He also engaged me in other restaurant projects such as The Great Eastern Hotel, and Sartoria. I learnt a huge amount about restaurant design, concept and development.

However, despite career opportunities and a bright future for me in London, my love affair with Australia never really ended.

Angela and I were ready to start a family and felt London wasn't the place to bring up young kids. We really did miss the high quality of life in Australia and so decided to relocate.

In 1998, I was appointed consulting Director of Food at the Sydney Opera House. Imagine how tough this gig was and how wide open I'd be to criticism! A 'know it all pom', fresh out of London, taking the helm at this iconic landmark! My brief was to change the direction, culture and philosophy of the food, giving particular attention to its flagship restaurant, Bennelong, enabling it to be more accessible to the people of Sydney and its visitors, particularly for the upcoming 2000 Olympics. I had mixed reviews, in fact I got panned by one critic, but despite this, the place was full and thriving and people were loving it. I was getting paid a fortune for this gig and knew it couldn't last.

I had spent the best part of 15 years working for other people and just wanted a restaurant of my own. I gathered our life savings and bought Pruniers in Woollahra, a landmark restaurant that had been part of Sydney's social elite for over 25 years, but at the time was a struggling Italian restaurant.

After a complete refurbishment, Pruniers was literally an overnight success and was awarded a chef's hat by the *Sydney Morning Herald* food reviewer, Terry Durack.

"The big night out is back...and the Eastern suburbs are loving it."

I was on a mission to conquer the world and soon after, I bought Bonne Femme (from good mate Matt Moran) a 60-seat restaurant in east Sydney, popular amongst foodies. Like Pruniers, it received a chef's hat from the *Sydney Morning Herald Good Food Guide*.

Despite their success, we didn't make any money and things were pretty tough. I was romanced by the the dot.com boom and thought I could make my fortune on the markets. But I lost the lot!

In 2002, I sold out of Pruniers and eventually closed Bonne Femme. Pretty much all our life savings had gone, but luckily I had established relationships in the industry, a world of experience and a head full of knowledge. I also had a great palate so could make big money as a consultant (thank goodness). At this point, I realised I could make more money in one day than any of my restaurants did in a week, so I decided to concentrate on this area and launched The Buzz Group. I had a great list of clients which included: Qantas, Singapore Airlines, British Airways, Birch and Waite, Accor Group, Sofitel Hotels and Resorts; Sanitarium, Vetta, Sumo Salads; Innovations/ Homecare, Domayne Homewares; Meat and Livestock Australia and Macquarie University.

A great opportunity came my way at Wildfire, one of Sydney's coolest and busiest new harbourside restaurants. I went in to set up operating systems in line with the Conran formula in London. I was comfortable being back running a big restaurant. Wildfire was the big night out in dining and I loved being back in the thick of it.

In 2005, The Accor Group were looking for a General Manager/Chef to rebuild the Summit's flagging reputation. I don't know why, but I found myself gravitating to iconic restaurants. It was the excitement of the challenge, I guess. Soon after settling into my new role, Accor promoted me to Group Director of Food for Sofitel Hotels and Resorts Australasia. I was still responsible for the Summit as well as overseeing and redeveloping all aspects of the food in seven five-star hotels. This was a dream job and would develop my career as a corporate chef. But I yearned to be back in the kitchen, on the front line, running a restaurant.

A very rare and almost impossible opportunity suddenly arose. Accor were starting to talk about putting the Summit up for sale. I was feeling pretty gutted about this, having worked so hard to deliver top quality food and service, leaving those buffet days a thing of the past. So after a few intense discussions and meetings with senior management, I came home one night and said to Angela, 'how do you fancy buying the Summit?' My mother-in-law was staying with us at the time and they both nearly fell off their seats. After eight months in negotiations, we bought it lock, stock and wine cellar.

Our life savings are now revolving 47 floors high above the city. From day one I have always instilled a rigorous approach to the Summit's food and service. Now that I have total freedom, I can make it my own. The location is truly world class and I am determined to continue taking this Sydney icon to new levels.

I take my culinary inspiration from the city and its people. I have a real passion for premium Australian produce and try to translate this into imaginative, superbly presented dishes that are underpinned by classic flavours.

I have really enjoyed writing this book. It contains some recipes that have been with me for years and while they have evolved over time, the principles of cookery remain true to the valuable training I gained in the very beginning.

Use this book to entertain your friends and family; either by cooking a fancy dinner or going for the simpler weekend brunch dishes.

I hope you become inspired and feel free to modify the recipes to suit your style. Go on, get your hands dirty and bring these dishes to life.

Remember this simple truth. Good food is a moment in time, but you will never find it if you don't look. Happy cooking.

THOUGHTS ON ENTERTAINING

There's so much *Moore to Food* when you are entertaining. Whether you are organising a casual catch up or hosting an impressive dinner, it's the extra elements that turn a great meal into a memorable one. Here are my tried and tested tips:

Planning is the key

Firstly, think about the end result you want to achieve. Plan well ahead, but be flexible and allow the party to evolve. Think in simple big brush strokes; is this a formal or casual meal? Shape every decision back to your original plans. Keep the food elegant and within your comfort zone.

The table and the menu

Try to make everyone comfortable and personalise the experience. As the host, there must be a little of you in everything. A written menu is such a nice touch, I like to get the kids to write it.

When setting the table do not clutter; try to think of what has to come onto the table and where it will go, choose your theme and follow it through. Candles are great for evening and flowers for the day. Keep the menu and each dish as simple as possible; no more than three flavours on a plate. You can still be creative by expanding the use of the same ingredient in the same dish.

Shopping

To cook good food consistently you'll need some good quality basic ingredients. Try to build a good pantry around the food style you like to cook. When shopping, be flexible and try not go with a fixed shopping list; be prepared to change to the best produce in season. Look in the shops a few days before or in books or magazines to stimulate some ideas . When planning I spend time talking to suppliers or looking at food in the markets and shops.

Food preparation

Start well ahead and precook what you can; remember you are a guest as well. Be prepared and remember a relaxed host equals happy guests.

Cooking

Try to relax, it will help you cook and present your best food. Do you have a dish you are really great at? Try and develop it. Both you and the dish should get better each time you come together.

Theatre

Around the meal, try to have some impressive surprises and original components, especially near the end. It can be as simple as some favourite chocolates or honeycomb with coffee or a homemade fruit chutney with cheese.

Serving the meal

Don't try to do everything yourself, ask someone for a helping hand before you start. I was my Mum's helper for years. It is important to get the food to the table hot and looking its best.

Cleaning up

Clean up at the beginning, middle and end. In my experience the hardest part of cooking a dinner party is when the entrées are being cleared to the kitchen and you are trying to serve the main course. Try to clear a space and plan where the dirty plates are going to go.

If you need to re-use a plate or some cutlery, have some hot soapy water and a clean cloth ready. Use ice cold water to cool it down before another course.

Kicking back and relaxing

As soon as you can, relax and enjoy the fruits of your labour. Unfortunately this can often be when everyone has left! It comes back to good planning remember! Your guests will feel more comfortable when you are.

Mistakes in your cooking?

This is important. Never admit to making a mistake in your cooking or preparation. You are really the only one who knows what you are trying to do and how you wanted the dish to look.

If something tastes bad, don't serve it. You can't hide the taste or smell of something that is burnt, never try to cover it up. Just leave it off the plate.

Finally, deliver everything with a smile and serve generously!

TAKE THE 'SENSE TEST'

The host's main role in entertaining is to engage everyone and get them relaxed and happy. As the host you set the framework, but the guests bring the party with them.

Whether I'm planning a casual or formal event, I have a mental checklist that I go through before I start. Over the years, it has served me well. I call it my 'Sense Test'.

So much of what we enjoy in life happens to us subconsciously, so in your planning consider the effect of what you do on your guests' senses. They are so easy to remember because we all have them and the good thing is they work for formal or casual events.

This is the order that I follow.

Sound

This is the first sense your guest will experience. It will also set the tone for the day.

First, select the music and the vibe you want. This is so important to get right. I like to get the music cranking early, especially when I am preparing at home. I never have music in the kitchen at work so this gets me in a different mind set and lets everyone know that there is going to be some fun. I like to have the music up high until the first guests arrive. If they walk in and hear you enjoying yourself you will be surprised how relaxed they become. Turn the music down immediately to allow conversation to start. From then on the music should only be in the background until the time comes to cut loose and party.

Smell

If music is first, smell is second. Put a great bunch of flowers or a scented candle near the front door or have them in the room. Open all the windows for 15 minutes.

Often friends will arrive with flowers as a gift. Put them into a vase immediately and on show.

The smells from baking and cooking are the best canapé you can serve. Many top restaurants around the world are including 'smell' in the dishes they serve. This can be smoke, citrus, garlic, or simply the warming of bread in the oven.

I like to serve something warm as a nibble to start. It can be as simple as olive toast to dip with rather than crackers.

Sight

Most guests will come to see you in the kitchen when they arrive, so always do a quick clean up just before they are due to turn up. This will really help you relax and give the impression that you are in control. It's not always easy, you could be stressed at this point, but try your best to relax—deep breath and a big smile! Then you can continue preparation.

This is the time to show fresh food. It can be an impressive fresh fruit basket, a bunch of herbs, fresh bread or the marinated lamb shoulder ready to go on the barbecue. Don't give it all away at the beginning—there needs to be an element of surprise as the meal goes forward.

Touch

A lot of guests like to become involved in the meal. They can open the wine or champagne. If someone brings a beautiful bottle of wine, make sure you open theirs to share.

Try my tapas-style nibbles. These allow your guests to start eating straight away. Sliced air dried hams or fresh dips are always good. If I see someone licking their fingers I know I am off to a good start.

Taste

Ultimately taste is the most important factor to entertaining and it has two aspects to it. First is your taste in presentation: the table, the food, yourself and the ambience of the room. Second is the flavour of the food. Taste everything you cook, check flavour constantly and correct the seasoning.

Temperatures are often miscalculated. Hot: we all know that main meals are served hot. Warm: I always serve my olives warm. Room temperature: marinated vegetables, tomatoes, dips, dressings and olives all taste better at room temperature. Cold: Shellfish and seafood must be served cold and chilled. Compile these just before serving or make up early and serve from the fridge. Chilled and crisp: all leaf salads must be chilled and crisp. Keep them covered with a damp cloth. A great tip is to turn your fridge temperature down the day before your party, as you will open it frequently on the day.

Give the Sense Test a go! The meal will just roll along from there.

BRUNCH

Brunch is a massive part of my weekend. Eating at home is a far less structured affair for me and a welcome escape from the restaurant. The following dishes can be eaten at any time during a lazy Saturday or Sunday. Some of them are very quick and simple, others take some forward planning.

RASPBERRY AND RICOTTA SOUFFLÉ PANCAKE

SERVES 4

150g (5oz) plain flour

½ teaspoon bicarbonate of soda

75g caster sugar

3 eggs, separated

300ml (10½fl oz) milk

Vegetable oil

200g (7oz) fresh full cream ricotta

1 x 150g (5oz) punnet fresh raspberries

2 tablespoons icing sugar

Thick cream or yoghurt to serve

Preheat grill on high heat.

Sift flour and bicarb soda into a large mixing bowl and mix in half the sugar; make a 'well' in the centre. Mix egg yolks and milk together and pour into flour. Slowly, whisk in milk to form a smooth batter; set aside.

Beat egg whites with electric beaters until soft peaks form, gradually add remaining sugar and beat until mixture becomes thick and glossy. Fold through pancake batter.

Warm a little oil in a small frying pan and pour in a quarter of the pancake mix; swirl to fill the whole pan. Randomly add 5 teaspoons of ricotta then sprinkle a handful of berries over the top; cook for 2 minutes on a low heat. Transfer to grill or hot oven and cook for 3 minutes or until mix has risen around the fruit. Place onto serving plates. Repeat with remaining mixture to make up the four pancakes.

Serve soufflé pancake with a good dusting of icing sugar and a dollop of thick cream or yoghurt.

CHAMPAGNE SUMMER BERRY BREAKFAST JELLY

SERVES 4-6

Soak gelatin leaves in cold water until completely softened.

Place 2 cups of champagne into a large saucepan and heat gently with sugar and orange slices until sugar dissolves. Remove from heat.

Squeeze excess water from gelatin and stir into champagne syrup until dissolved. Add remaining champagne and mix well.

Mix the fruit together and divide among 4-6 martini or serving glasses. Pour over warm champagne syrup. Fruit will rise to the top. Refrigerate until jelly has set.

Serve chilled with lightly whipped cream or yoghurt.

4 sheets of Titanium or gold gelatin leaves

1 x 750ml (75cl) bottle champagne or sparkling wine

125g (4½oz) caster sugar

1 orange, cut into thick slices

2 x punnets raspberries

1 x punnet strawberries, hulled and halved

1 x punnet blueberries

Fresh thick Greek yoghurt or whipped cream to serve

BIRCHER MUESLI WITH HONEY YOGHURT, PASSIONFRUIT AND APPLE SALAD

SERVES 4–6

Nut topping

60g (2oz) pumpkin seeds

60g (2oz) sunflower seeds

30g (1oz) sesame seeds

60g (2oz) slivered almonds

150g (5oz) organic rolled oats

250ml (9fl oz) buttermilk

150ml (5fl oz) milk

100ml (3½fl oz) good quality or fresh squeezed apple juice

2 ripe bananas

2 tablespoons leatherwood honey

¼ teaspoon vanilla paste or 1 fresh pod, scraped

1 tablespoon brown sugar

Zest of half a lemon

1 tablespoon lemon juice

1 green (granny smith) apple

Apple salad

1 red crispy (royal gala) apple

200g (7oz) honey vanilla yoghurt to serve

2 fresh passionfruit, cut in half and pulped

Preheat oven to 180°C (350°F) and line a baking tray with baking paper. Scatter nut topping onto tray and bake for 10 minutes, or until toasted and brown. Cool and set aside.

To make the bircher muesli, combine oats, buttermilk, milk, and apple juice. Mash the bananas in a bowl with a table fork and stir in the honey, vanilla paste, brown sugar, lemon zest and juice; mix well. Pour into oat mixture, cover and refrigerate overnight.

Just before serving, grate granny smith apple on a cheese grater and stir through the oat mixture. Adjust sweetness to taste and consistency with a little more milk or apple juice.

To serve, cut the apple into thin strips the size of matchsticks, spoon the bircher muesli into serving glasses, add a dollop of honey yoghurt then sprinkle some of the prepared nut seed mix over the top. Top with apple salad and a squeeze of the fresh-cut passionfruit pulp.

SMOOTH DOUBLE CREAM SCRAMBLED EGGS WITH SMOKED TROUT

SERVES 4

12 fresh eggs

Sea salt and white pepper

100ml (3½fl oz) double cream

40g (1½oz) butter, softened

300g (10½oz) smoked trout, picked free of skin and bones

1 bunch chives, finely chopped

Soy and linseed bread, toasted

Freshly ground black pepper

Crack eggs into a glass bowl, mix well and season well with salt and pepper. Stir in cream and butter.

Bring a saucepan of water to the boil and place the bowl of eggs over it to make a bain marie. Take care that the bottom of the bowl does not touch the boiling water.

Using a wooden spoon, stir the eggs slowly. This will take a few minutes, but gradually the eggs will start to cook. Continue to stir. Do not allow eggs to cook on the side of the bowl—eggs must look creamy and silky.

Once the eggs have started to thicken, remove from heat and stir through the trout. Adjust seasoning and add the chopped chives.

To serve, spoon scrambled eggs over hot buttered toast and offer freshly ground black pepper at the table.

COLD SET CHICKEN, ARTICHOKE AND CHICKPEA SALAD WITH MAYONNAISE

SERVES 4-6

Place chicken in a large saucepan with the water, onion, garlic, parsley, peppercorns and salt. Bring to the boil and simmer for 40 minutes. Test that chicken is cooked by inserting a knife into the thigh. If the juices are clear then chicken is ready to remove from heat.

Carefully remove chicken from the hot water and plunge into a large container of iced water; this will set the juices in the flesh of the chicken and ensure that it stays moist and juicy. Cool chicken completely in iced water.

While the chicken is cooling, prepare the chickpeas by cooking them in a pan of boiling water for 1 hour or until completely tender. Drain and cool.

Toast almonds in a frying pan or in a hot oven until lightly browned.

Combine lemon juice, olive oil, sugar, salt and pepper in bowl and whisk together.

Add chickpeas, artichokes, parsley, almonds and preserved lemon and toss gently to mix well.

In a separate bowl, carefully shred chicken flesh into thin strips and mix through with mayonnaise to coat and moisten chicken. Season to taste.

To serve, place artichoke and chickpea salad onto the side of a serving platter and spoon chicken next to it, with crusty fresh bread.

1.2kg (2½lb) whole organic chicken

2 litres (3½ pints) water

1 onion, quartered

1 garlic bulb, cut in half

4 parsley stalks

1 teaspoon whole black peppercorns

1 teaspoon sea salt

100g (3½oz) dried chickpeas, soaked overnight in water

60g (2oz) blanched almonds

Juice of 1 lemon

80ml (3oz) extra virgin olive oil

Pinch sugar

Salt and freshly ground black pepper

400g (1lb) marinated artichokes, quartered

½ bunch flat-leaf parsley, leaves picked

1 piece preserved lemon, rinsed and sliced thinly

1 quantity of olive oil mayonnaise (see Basics)

GRILLED FIGS AND STONE FRUIT WITH RICOTTA AND TOAST

SERVES 4-6

100g (3½oz) butter

60g (2oz) brown sugar

60g (2oz) honey

Pinch ground cinnamon

Pinch ground ginger

½ teaspoon vanilla bean paste

12 small plums (Angelina or sugar), halved with stone removed

4 fresh green figs, halved

2 ripe white nectarines, stone removed and quartered

500g (17½oz) very fresh full cream ricotta in basket or pack

Toasted sourdough to serve

Place butter, sugar, honey, spices and vanilla into a small saucepan and heat gently over medium heat until sugar has dissolved.

Mix fruit together in a large bowl and pour over the sugar syrup, toss to coat evenly.

Preheat a grill and cook fruit in batches until caramelised and softened. Pour any remaining syrup in the bowl over the warm grilled fruit.

Invert the ricotta pack or basket onto a serving plate and top with the warm fruit, allowing syrup and fruit to tumble down the sides. Place in the centre of table and serve immediately with toasted sourdough.

Alternatively, spread ricotta onto warm grilled toast and serve individually.

You may substitute any fruit in season, such as pears, berries and sugar bananas.

BAKED EGGS WITH SMOKEY ROASTED CAPSICUM, BEANS AND CHORIZO

SERVES 4

Preheat oven to 220°C (430°F). Line a baking tray with baking paper. Place capsicums onto tray and roast for 30 minutes, turning capsicums over half way. Once the skins have blistered and blackened, remove and cover with a clean tea towel and cool. Reduce oven temperature to 180°C (350°F).

Peel and deseed the capsicums and place into a blender with the garlic, almonds and red wine vinegar. Pulse to a paste then add smoked paprika, lemon juice and zest, and drizzle in olive oil until a thick sauce is formed. Season to taste.

Heat a large frying pan over a medium/high heat and add chorizo; cook for 2-3 minutes or until fat from sausage starts melting into pan. Add onion and cannellini beans and cook for a further 3 minutes. Stir in roasted capsicum relish and cook for 10 minutes or until sauce is thick.

Spoon the mixture into a medium glass or ceramic baking dish, pushing the mixture to the sides to make space for the eggs. Break the eggs into the space and drizzle a little extra olive oil over the top.

Bake for 8-10 minutes, or until the eggs are cooked to your liking. Season with freshly ground black pepper.

Break up cheese over the hot baked eggs, sprinkle with some chopped parsley and serve with toasted ciabatta bread.

Roasted capsicum relish

3 red capsicums (peppers)

1 clove garlic

80g (3oz) blanched whole almonds

60ml (2fl oz) red wine vinegar

1 teaspoon smoked Spanish paprika

Juice and zest of a lemon

200ml (7fl oz) olive oil

Sea salt and pepper

2 chorizo sausages, sliced across

1 onion, finely diced

300g (10½oz) cooked cannellini beans or chickpeas

4 large eggs

Extra virgin olive oil

150g (5oz) mozzarella or fresh ricotta cheese

2 tablespoons chopped flat parsley

1 ciabatta loaf, sliced and toasted

ROASTED MUSHROOM AND ONION SOUP WITH THE BEST GARLIC AND PARMESAN BREAD

SERVES 4-6

Preheat oven to 180°C (350°F). Place mushrooms, onion, garlic, thyme into a roasting tray. Over the top of the vegetables, scatter diced butter and 1½ tablespoons (20ml) of olive oil. Season with salt and pepper and roast in oven for 35-40 minutes or until mushrooms and onions have softened and caramelised.

Heat remaining oil in a large saucepan over medium/high heat and add roasted onion, mushroom and pan juices to pan; cook, stirring for 2-3 minutes. Stir in porcini powder and white wine and cook for a further 1-2 minutes or until alcohol has evaporated. Add in stock, reduce heat and simmer for 20 minutes. Purée soup with a blender until smooth. Return soup to pan and bring back to the simmer. Add cream and season to taste.

Place garlic halves, cut side down, onto an oiled roasting tray and roast for 40 minutes in oven until softened and caramelised. Remove and cool before squeezing out roasted garlic flesh from the skin. Mash in a bowl and season with salt and pepper. Stir through softened butter and chopped parsley then set aside.

Slice the loaf half way down from the top, keeping the base of the loaf intact. Push garlic butter into the cuts and then sprinkle parmesan into the slices and then over the top of the loaf. Place onto a baking tray and bake for 15 minutes or until cheese has melted and bread is crisp.

Ladle soup into warmed soup bowls and serve with garlic parmesan loaf; tear off slices as required.

1kg (2lb) mixed mushrooms, such as field, button, Swiss brown and oyster mushrooms

400g (¾lb) small brown onions, peeled and quartered

3 cloves garlic, halved

3-4 sprigs fresh thyme

50g (1¾oz) butter, diced

60ml (2fl oz) olive oil

Salt and pepper

1 teaspoon porcini powder

250ml (9fl oz) white wine

1.5 litres (2½ pints) chicken stock

250ml (9fl oz) cream

Garlic and parmesan bread

3 bulbs garlic, cut in half, skins on

275g (9oz) softened butter

1 large sourdough loaf

1 tablespoon chopped parsley

100g (3½oz) parmesan, grated

SLOW-COOKED CHICKEN, ORZO PASTA AND WHITE BEANS

SERVES 4

This dish is perfect if you want to skip breakfast and go straight to an early lunch. It takes five minutes to prepare and one hour to cook. I use a chicken 'brick' which you can see in the following photographs.

500g (1lb) small carrots, trimmed

2 whole small leeks

2 onions, peeled and diced

1 bay leaf

30g butter

1 sprig of fresh thyme

125ml (4½fl oz) dry white wine

2kg (4½lb) organic chicken, trimmed of excess fat.

2 lemons

3 tablespoons (40ml) olive oil

200g (4 oz) cooked orzo pasta

200g (4oz) cooked cannellini beans

1 quantity of walnut pesto (see Basics)

Preheat oven to 180°C (350°F). Arrange vegetables, herbs, wine and 1 cup of water into the base of a chicken brick or deep roasting dish that has a lid.

Wash chicken thoroughly, making sure that the cavity is free of blood and organs; pat dry with paper towel. Slice one lemon thinly and tuck under the skin with herbs and some butter. Quarter the remaining lemon and fill the cavity. Rub oil over chicken skin and season with salt and pepper.

Place the chicken on top of the vegetables.

Cover with lid and roast in a medium oven. After 45 minutes, remove lid, and baste chicken with pan juices. Return chicken to oven, uncovered and cook a further 20 minutes or until skin is golden and juices run clear when the thigh is pierced with a skewer near the bone.

Remove from oven and cut chicken into serving portions, cover with foil and keep warm. Roughly chop the hot vegetables and return to the dish, stir in the orzo pasta and the cannellini beans, mix well with the juices. Heat well and adjust the seasoning

To serve, spoon pasta and vegetables onto a plates and top with chicken and a dollop of walnut pesto.

MY ONE-POT, ONE-BOWL CRAB NAPOLITANO PASTA

SERVES 4

1kg (2lbs) ripe tomatoes (Roma), halved lengthways

2 teaspoons caster sugar

Sea salt and pepper to taste

2 cloves garlic, thinly sliced

1 medium red chilli, sliced

2 sprigs fresh thyme

80ml (3oz) extra virgin olive oil

400g (¾lb) tagliatelle or spaghetti

150g (5oz) picked fresh crab meat

Parmesan to serve

Preheat oven to 220°C (430°F) and line a baking tray with baking paper. Place tomatoes onto tray, cut side up, and sprinkle over sugar, salt and pepper. Place a slice of garlic and red chilli on each tomato. Rub thyme between hands and sprinkle over randomly. Drizzle over 2 tablespoons of oil and roast for 30 minutes or until softened and almost collapsed. This will concentrate the tomato flavour.

Remove from oven and chop tomatoes coarsely on a board with a large knife. Tip into a large metal bowl along with all the juices from tray and crush slightly.

Meanwhile, bring a large pot of salted water to the boil; add tagliatelle or spaghetti and cook for 12 minutes or until al dente.

While pasta is cooking, place metal bowl of tomatoes over simmering water. Remove bowl and drain pasta, reserving ½ cup of cooking water. Transfer the hot pasta to the tomatoes and add crab; mix well to coat evenly. If pasta is too dry, add a spoonful of hot cooking water to loosen up sauce.

Season to taste and serve topped with freshly grated parmesan.

RARE ROAST BEEF SANDWICH WITH GORGONZOLA AND PEAR SALAD

SERVES 4-6

Preheat oven to 180°C (350°F).

Place thyme, garlic, salt and pepper into a mortar and pestle and grind to a paste. Add oil and mix well. Rub evenly over beef fillet.

Heat a non-stick frying pan over a high heat and fry the beef, until sealed and golden on all sides. Transfer to the oven and cook for a further 15 minutes. Remove and rest, loosely covered with foil to keep warm.

Mix sliced pears and rocket leaves together in a bowl. Whisk lemon juice and oil together; season with salt and pepper and drizzle over the salad. Toss to coat evenly.

Slice warm beef thinly and pile onto the sliced bread; top with pear and rocket salad and crumble over the gorgonzola cheese. Top with remaining slice of bread.

1 tablespoon chopped fresh thyme

2 cloves garlic

Salt and pepper

2 tablespoons olive oil

1kg (2lbs) beef fillet, trimmed and tied

2 beurre bosc pears, core removed and finely sliced

80g (3oz) baby rocket leaves or picked watercress

2 tablespoons lemon juice

1 tablespoon extra virgin olive oil

1 large sourdough loaf, cut into 8 thick slices

150g (5oz) gorgonzola piquant blue cheese

Fish cakes

800g (1½lb) salmon fillet, pin boned and skin removed

1 tablespoon caster sugar

1 tablespoon sea salt

Poaching bouillon

1 carrot, chopped

1 onion, sliced

5 bay leaves

3–4 parsley stalks

1 leek, white part only, sliced

1 teaspoon black peppercorns

Large pinch of salt

500ml (¾pint) water

700g (1½ lb) potato, peeled and diced

1 red onion, finely chopped

1 long red chilli, finely chopped

2 tablespoons finely chopped Italian parsley

100g (3½oz) plain flour

2 eggs, lightly beaten

80g (3oz) dried breadcrumbs

Oil for shallow frying

1 quantity of roasted tomato jam (see Basics)

Potato chips

1kg (2lb) desiree potatoes, peeled

Oil for deepfrying

Sea salt

Malt vinegar to serve

SALT-CURED SALMON FISH CAKES WITH HAND-CUT CHIPS AND MALT VINEGAR

SERVES 4

These fishcakes take a little while to prepare, but they are a great way to get the children involved in the kitchen.

Place salmon fillet in a shallow dish, skin down, and sprinkle the sugar and salt over the flesh side of the fish. Cover and refrigerate for at least 2 hours.

To make poaching bouillon, place carrot, onion, bay leaves, parsley stalks, leek, peppercorns, salt and water in a deep pan. Bring to the boil and simmer for 15 minutes with a lid on.

Remove salmon from refrigerator and brush off excess salt and sugar. Place carefully into poaching bouillon and simmer for 2 minutes with lid on. Remove pan from heat and allow to cool. Remove fish from poaching liquid and flake into a large bowl. Add cooled tomato jam, mix well and refrigerate for up to 2 hours to marinate. Discard poaching liquid.

Cook potatoes in boiling water until softened; drain and mash until smooth. Cool completely.

To make the fish cakes, add the mashed potato, onion, chilli, parsley and seasoning to the salmon mixture and mix well with your hands. Divide fish cake mixture into 8 portions and shape into large patties. Refrigerate for 30 minutes.

Flour, egg and breadcrumb the fishcake and pan fry in hot oil for 2–3 minutes each side or until crisp and golden.

To make the potato chips, trim potatoes into a 10cm (4in) long x 1cm (½in) wide chips. Wash and pat dry thoroughly. Heat a large wok or deep saucepan half full of vegetable oil to 160°C (320°F) and cook potatoes in batches for 3 minutes. Remove and drain and repeat until all chips have been blanched. Increase heat to 190°C (370°F) and return chips to oil; cook until golden and crisp. Drain on absorbent paper and sprinkle with sea salt.

Serve fish cakes with hot chips and a small dish of malt vinegar.

CANAPÉS

Canapés come in many forms and they set the tone of the meal to follow. Simple warm olives are the easiest way to impress, the flavour is surprisingly released by some gentle heat.

OYSTERS WITH CUCUMBER TEA GRANITA

6 SERVINGS, 2 OYSTERS PER PERSON

Choose the freshest oysters you can find. I like the clean saltwater flavour of Pacifics. They taste even better if you open them yourself.

8 cucumbers, peeled and chopped

2 teaspoons sea salt

Freshly ground pepper

Juice and zest of a lemon

1 chilli, finely chopped

1 teaspoon fish sauce

12 freshly shucked oysters

Finely shredded cucumber for garnish

To make the cucumber tea granita, place cucumbers in a food processor and process until coarsely chopped. Tip into a bowl and season with salt and pepper. Pour over lemon juice and zest and allow to stand in fridge for ½ hour. Strain through a fine strainer, collecting the green liquid in a bowl. Add chilli and fish sauce and mix well. Pour into a shallow dish, cover and freeze for 2 hours.

Once frozen, scrape the top with a fork to create small ice crystals.

Place the freshly opened oysters onto serving platters and spoon a little of the iced cucumber tea granita and finely shredded cucumber with some chilli on the top.

Serve immediately.

OYSTERS WITH PICKLED TOMATO GRANITA

6 SERVINGS, 2 OYSTERS PER PERSON

To make the pickled tomato granita, bring a pan of water to the boil. Make a cross-shaped incision into the base of each tomato and plunge into the boiling water, cook for 3 minutes and remove. Place into a bowl of ice water and cool completely. Peel skin off tomatoes and cut in half.

Place the tomatoes into a dish and pour over vinegar, sugar, basil and seasoning. Stand for 30 minutes, turning tomatoes over half way.

Line a fine sieve with muslin cloth and place over a glass bowl. Crush tomatoes with clean hands, making sure to break up flesh and seeds. Pile tomato mixture into sieve and push gently down with a spoon to release tomato juice.

Pour juice into a shallow dish, cover and freeze for 2 hours. Once frozen, scrape the top with a fork to create small ice crystals.

Cut baby tomatoes in half and soften in a warm oven. Place freshly shucked oysters onto a platter and place a small teaspoon of granita onto each oyster. Garnish with the baby tomato halves.

Serve immediately.

4 ripe vine-ripened tomatoes

60ml (2fl oz) chardonnay vinegar

2 teaspoons sugar

2 baby tomatoes

1 bunch fresh basil, leaves picked

Sea salt and pepper

12 freshly shucked oysters

From left clockwise: pickled cucumber granita, cabernet mignonette granita, pickled tomato granita.

OYSTERS WITH CABERNET MIGNONETTE GRANITA

6 SERVINGS, 2 OYSTERS PER PERSON

50ml (3½ tablespoons) good quality white wine vinegar

100ml (3½fl oz) red wine (cabernet) vinegar

60ml (4 tablespoons) water

1 teaspoon sugar

2 eschallots, finely chopped

Sea salt and pepper

½ punnet baby red chard leaves

12 freshly shucked oysters

To make the cabernet mignonette granita, combine vinegars, sugar, shallots and mix well; allow to stand for 30 minutes. Strain through a fine sieve into a small shallow dish, cover and freeze for 2 hours.

Once frozen, scrape the top with a fork to create small ice crystals.

Place oysters onto a platter and place a small teaspoon of granita onto each oyster. Garnish with baby red chard leaves.

Serve immediately.

WATERMELON AND GINGER OYSTER SHOTS

SERVES 6

Blend watermelon, ginger, mint, cucumber and water together in a food processor or blender until smooth. Strain through a fine strainer and taste; adjust seasoning with salt and lime juice.

Place a freshly shucked oyster in the base of the shot glasses and top each one with some of the watermelon gazpacho.

Garnish with a stick of cucumber and a mint leaf.

Serve immediately.

200g (7oz) watermelon flesh, chopped

1 tablespoon grated fresh ginger

2 tablespoons chopped mint leaves

½ cucumber, peeled and deseeded

40ml (3 tablespoons) water

Sea salt and lime juice to taste

12 freshly shucked oysters

Cucumber sticks and mint leaves for garnish

POTATO PANCAKES WITH MANDARIN VODKA-CURED SALMON, HERBED CRÉME FRAÎCHE

MAKES 24 SMALL PANCAKES

Cut salmon in half across-ways and lay, skin side down, on a large sheet of plastic wrap.

Combine salt, sugar, dill, citrus and vodka together and mix well. Press dill mixture onto flesh side of one piece of salmon. Cover with second piece of salmon, skin side up. Wrap tightly with plastic wrap and place into a shallow dish; refrigerate for 12 hours.

Remove salmon from fridge and drain off any liquids; rewrap, turn salmon over and refrigerate for a further 12 hours. Remove salmon from plastic and scrape away curing mix. Lightly rinse under cold water then pat dry with a cloth; refrigerate until required.

To make the potato pancakes, combine the eggs, milk, flour and bicarbonate of soda in a mixing bowl. Add the potato and mix well. Season with salt and pepper. Heat a little oil in a large non-stick frying pan and spoon tablespoons of pancake mixture to pan; cook for 1–2 minutes each side or until golden and cooked through. Remove and drain on absorbent paper.

Mix crème fraîche with other ingredients in a small bowl and season to taste.

To serve, finely slice cured salmon on the diagonal; place onto potato pancakes, fill with herbed crème fraîche and a small amount of salmon roe.

Marinated vodka-cured salmon

500g (1lb) fresh salmon, skin on, pin-boned

60g (2oz) sea salt

60g (2oz) caster sugar

½ cup chopped fresh dill

Zest of a large mandarin

Zest of a lemon

80ml (3oz) Citron vodka

60g (2oz) salmon roe

Potato pancakes

2 eggs

125ml (4½fl oz) milk

2 tablespoons self-raising flour

Pinch bicarbonate of soda

1 large desiree potato, boiled, peeled and grated

Salt and pepper

Oil for shallow frying

Herb crème fraîche

300ml crème fraîche

1½ tablespoons (20ml) vodka

1 tablespoon lemon juice

2 tablespoons chopped dill

2 tablespoons chopped parsley

CRISP-FRIED PRAWNS WITH SOMIN NOODLES

SERVES 6-8

You can buy these noodles from Asian supermarkets or delicatessens.

3 nori sheets,
cut into 20cm x 4cm (12in x 2in) strips

200g (7oz) dried somin noodles

18 medium green prawns, peeled and deveined

Oil for deep frying

Soy and mirin dipping sauce

60ml (2fl oz) Japanese light soy

60ml (2fl oz) mirin

2 teaspoons sugar

2 teaspoons grated ginger

1 green onion, finely sliced

1 small red chilli, seeds removed and finely chopped

Mix soy, mirin and sugar together until sugar has dissolved. Add remaining ingredients and pour into a small dipping bowl.

Place a strip of nori onto a flat work surface and cover with a single layer of dried somin noodles. Place a green prawn into the centre of each one and roll the noodles to form a tube. Seal with a spot of water on the nori strip.

Half fill a wok or saucepan with oil and heat over high heat. Deep-fry prawn parcels in batches for 4 minutes, or until noodles are golden and crisp and the prawn is cooked through. Drain on absorbent paper.

Cut prawn nori bundles in half through the centre and stand, cut side down, on platter; serve immediately with dipping sauce.

WET-CURED OCEAN TROUT AND HIRIMASA KINGFISH, VANILLA SPIKED WITH CITRUS DRESSING

MAKES 36 CANAPES

These are a tasty alternative to traditional smoked salmon.

In a tray, place the rock salt and the chopped dill then add the zest of 2 oranges, lime and lemon, and squeeze their juice onto the salt. Add a generous amount of freshly ground pepper.

Split the vanilla pods and scrap the seeds into the salt mix.

Lay the fish fillets on a board and remove any small bones, place the split vanilla pods onto the fish.

Place the fish fillets directly into the salt mixture and cover well. Leave in the salt mix for 20–30 minutes, remove and lightly wash under cold water. Pat dry and slice thinly (you may leave the fish fillets whole for up to 24 hours).

In a small bowl place some mayonnaise, then grate in some orange, lime and lemon zest. Add a little juice and adjust the seasoning.

To serve, spread a little of the dressing onto the toasted crostini, slice the fish thinly, garnish with some baby lettuce leaves and some ocean trout roes, drizzle with a little olive oil before serving.

200g (7oz) rock salt

1 bunch dill

2 oranges

1 lime

1 lemon

Freshly ground black pepper

2 vanilla beans

1 side ocean trout

1 side kingfish
approx 800g (1 ½lb) each

100ml (3 ½fl oz) mayonnaise

Sliced baguettes rubbed with olive oil/ pepper then baked crisp

2 punnets baby lettuce leaves

90g (3oz) ocean trout roes

60ml (2 fl oz) extra virgin olive oil

RARE VEAL AND FENNEL INVOLTINI

SERVES 8–10

1kg (2lb) veal loin

Sea salt and pepper

2 tablespoons olive oil

3 baby fennel, trimmed and finely sliced into thin strips

5 green onions, trimmed and finely sliced into thin strips

½ bunch young celery

2 pears, peeled and sliced

2 bunches garlic chives, trimmed

Mayonnaise

3 egg yolks

1 teaspoon Dijon mustard, plus extra 2 teaspoons

2 teaspoons lemon juice

100ml (3½fl oz) extra virgin olive oil

150ml (5fl oz) sunflower oil

1 clove garlic, crushed

Raw small radishes to garnish

Preheat oven to 160°C (320°F) and season veal well with salt and pepper.

Heat oil in a large frying pan over medium/high heat and seal veal evenly on all sides until golden brown. Transfer to a baking dish and roast in oven for 15 minutes, making sure veal is very rare. Remove from oven, cool and refrigerate until completely cold.

To make the mayonnaise, whisk egg yolks, half the mustard and lemon juice together until smooth. Slowly drizzle in oils, a little at a time, while continuously whisking. Spoon ½ cup of mayonnaise into a bowl and stir in garlic and extra mustard. Season to taste.

Slice cold veal thinly, across the grain and place slices on lined trays. Spread ½ teaspoon of mayonnaise mixture over each slice and season with salt and pepper.

Bundle a few strips of fennel, green onion, pear, celery and chives and place along one end of the veal slice. The vegetables should overhang on one end only. Roll up to enclose vegetables in a neat roll and place in fridge until serving.

To serve, stand stacks on platter with the fresh-cut vegetables uppermost.

Serve with cold raw fresh garden radishes and sea salt.

BUFFALO MOZZARELLA WITH TOMATO ON TOAST AND BLACK OLIVE TAPENADE

SERVES 6-8

Black olive tapenade

200g (7oz) pitted Kalamata olives, chopped

2 cloves garlic, crushed

1 tablespoon salted capers, rinsed and drained

3 salted high-quality anchovies, chopped

1 sprig fresh lemon thyme leaves

60ml (2fl oz) olive oil

2 thin sourdough baguettes, cut into 1cm thick slices

1 clove garlic

2 tablespoons extra virgin olive oil, plus extra for brushing onto bread

2 large ripe ox heart tomatoes

1 tablespoon chopped continental parsley

Sea salt and pepper

3 x100g (3½oz) buffalo mozzarella cheese

Small fresh basil leaves to garnish

Place olives, 1 clove of garlic, capers, anchovies and thyme into the bowl of a food processor and pulse until broken down but not smooth. While still pulsing processor, drizzle in oil until well combined; spoon into a bowl, cover and refrigerate until needed.

Preheat oven to 180°C (350°F). Place bread slices onto baking trays, rub with a cut clove of raw garlic and brush both sides with olive oil; toast in oven for 4-5 minutes or until crisp. Turn slices over and cook a further 2-3 minutes. Remove and cool.

Grate the tomatoes on a cheese grater into a bowl, add olive oil, parsley and season with salt and pepper.

To serve, spread tapenade over each slice and top with a spoonful of tomato and a torn piece of fresh mozzarella; drizzle with remaining olive oil and serve.

Garnish with fresh basil leaves.

COLD-SMOKED HIRIMASA KINGFISH WITH SPICED MISO DRESSING

SERVES 6

Combine miso paste with sugar and salt and stir in enough water to form a spreadable paste. Brush cut surface of kingfish evenly with miso paste mixture; cover and refrigerate for ½ hour.

For the smoking, line a wok with double layers of foil and combine smoking mixture. Tip into the base of wok and fit a greased wire rack over the top. Turn heat on low.

And allow the smoke to begin and burn off for 5 minutes.

Place kingfish onto the rack, and cover with the wok lid. Remove wok from heat and allow to stand, lightly smoking for 12 minutes. Remove fish, cover and cool and slice thinly.

For the miso dressing, combine all ingredients in a blender and process until smooth. Pour into a sealed container and refrigerate until required.

To serve, spoon a little of the miso dressing onto an Asian spoon; roll kingfish slices and place onto spoons, garnish with baby herbs.

150g (5oz) white miso paste

1 tablespoon sugar

1 teaspoon sea salt

800g (1¾lbs) side Hirimasa kingfish, pin-boned and skin off

Smoking mixture

100g (3½oz) raw rice

60g (2oz) brown sugar

60g (2oz) green tea leaves

2 pieces dried orange peel

2 sticks lemongrass, trimmed and bruised

Miso dressing

1 teaspoon finely grated ginger

100g (3½oz) silken tofu

60g (2oz) white miso paste

125ml (4½fl oz) fresh orange juice

2 teaspoons brown sugar

2 teaspoons light soy sauce

2 tablespoons rice vinegar

2 teaspoons sesame oil

Baby coriander or shisho leaves for garnish

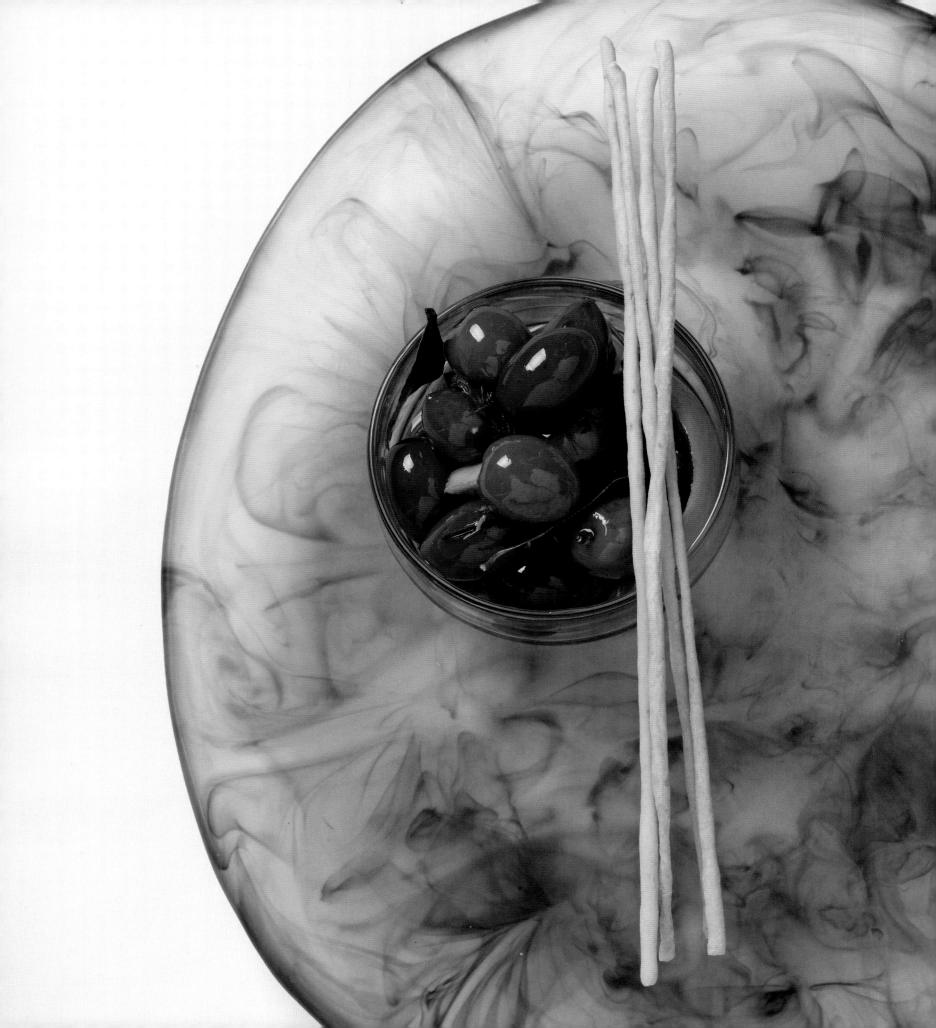

WARM ROASTED OLIVES, FENNEL AND HERBS, HANDROLLED BREAD STICKS

SERVES 6-8

Preheat oven to 200°C (390°F) and add oil, garlic, fennel seeds, bay leaves, thyme and orange rind into a deep baking dish. Place into oven and heat for 10 minutes or until oil is boiling. Stir in olives and return to oven; roast for a further 15 minutes, stirring halfway through the cooking time. Remove from oven and keep warm. Alternatively, cool completely and store in refrigerator in a sealed container until required.

To make the bread sticks, combine yeast, sugar and water together and mix well; stand for 5 minutes to activate the yeast. Once bubbles have appeared on the surface of the water it is ready to use. Place flour and salt into a large mixing bowl and make a well in the centre; add olive oil and yeast mixture and mix well to a soft dough. Tip onto a lightly floured work surface and knead for 5 minutes or until smooth and elastic. Return to bowl; cover and stand in a warm place to double in size (this could take about an hour). Knock back dough and knead again until smooth. Divide dough into 4 pieces.

Turn oven down to 180°C (350°F) and line two baking trays with baking paper.

Roll out one portion of dough to 1cm (½in) thickness. Cut long thin strips and roll on the bench to a grissini shape, dust with a little flour. Place grissini onto trays; bake until golden and crisp. Repeat with remaining dough.

To serve, spoon warm olives into serving bowls and serve with crisp bread sticks.

200ml (7fl oz) olive oil

5 whole garlic cloves, unpeeled

2 teaspoons fennel seeds

2 small bay leaves

4-5 fresh thyme leaves

3 strips of orange rind, pith removed

500g (1lbs) mixed olives (Ligurian, Sicilian, black olives, Kalamata)

Handrolled bread sticks

1 sachet (7g) dried yeast

1 teaspoon sugar

100ml (3½fl oz) lukewarm water

1 teaspoon sea salt

150g (5oz) strong plain flour, plus extra for kneading

20ml (1½ tablespoons) olive oil

ENTRÉES

Entrées are a great way to get your creative juices flowing. I could have written a whole book on this subject. Many of my friends prefer to eat two entrées, rather than a traditional three-course meal. This trend is a reflection on our society; we are not as hungry anymore and often eating is seen as a social interaction and an exploration of flavours. Many tapas lounges have become popular as they serve a large variety of small plates.

SASHIMI TUNA WITH SCORCHED ORANGE DRESSING

SERVES 6

Combine shallots and green chilli in a bowl.

Slice skin off orange in large pieces and set aside. Juice orange and strain over French shallots and chilli. Add lemon juice, vinegar and pepper and mix well; stand for ½ hour. Whisk in oil and season with salt.

Finely slice 1 piece of orange peel into long thin strips, making sure that there is no pith; reserve for garnish.

Fire the remaining orange peel by heating orange peel with gas lighter or burner over dressing and crushing peel simultaneously in your hand; squeeze out orange oil and mix into dressing. Continue until all of the peel has been fired.

To serve, trim skin and blood line from tuna then cut into neat blocks. Cut blocks into 1 cm (½ in) thick slices and place onto a long platter. Drizzle over dressing and garnish with finely sliced orange peel.

700g – 1 kg (1 ½ – 2 lb) sashimi grade tuna or Hirimasa kingfish

Scorched orange dressing

3 French shallots, very finely diced

2 medium green chillies, seeded and finely chopped

1 large orange

1 ½ tablespoons lemon juice

1 ½ tablespoons chardonnay vinegar

1 pinch freshly finely ground black pepper

100ml (3 ½ fl oz) extra virgin olive oil

Sea salt to taste

PRAWN MINESTRONE WITH WALNUT PESTO

SERVES 6

12 medium green prawns

1 medium red chilli, halved

1 clove garlic, quartered

300ml (10fl oz) tomato passata

1 tablespoon of tomato paste

1 tablespoon olive oil

1 small white onion, finely chopped

1 medium green zucchini (courgette), finely diced

2 Roma tomatoes, finely diced

1 baby fennel, finely diced

1 stick celery, finely diced

150ml (5fl oz) white wine

300g (10½oz) cooked cannellini beans

Salt and white pepper

1 quantity of walnut pesto (see Basics)

1 bunch basil leaves, chopped

60g (2oz) grated parmesan

Peel and devein prawns, leaving the tails intact. Remove the heads and place prawn heads and shells, chilli and garlic into a bowl and pour over 1.5 litres boiling water. Add tomato passata and a tablespoon of tomato paste and microwave for 3 minutes. Remove and allow to stand for 10 minutes. Strain through a fine sieve, crushing prawns to extract as much of the flavour as possible. Discard shells and set stock aside.

Heat oil in a large pan over medium heat and add onion, zucchini, tomato, fennel and celery. Cook gently for 3–4 minutes, or until softened but not coloured. Stir in wine and reserved stock and bring to the boil. Reduce heat to low and simmer for 10 minutes.

Stir through cannellini beans and simmer a further 5 minutes. Season with salt and pepper. Remove soup from heat and add prawns. Stand for 5 minutes or until prawns are cooked through.

In the restaurant, we prepare this stage using glass tubes to stand the prawns in the ministrone.

Make walnut pesto and add extra basil leaves and parmesan. Season well and set aside.

To serve, reheat and divide minestrone amongst six large serving bowls. Top with a dollop of pesto and serve with fresh bread.

SUMMER BEEF CARPACCIO AND CAESAR SALAD

SERVES 4

200g (7oz) piece beef fillet, trimmed and denuded

4 quail eggs

White vinegar

1 baby cos, trimmed and cut into quarters

1 tablespoon salted baby capers, rinsed and drained

50g Reggiano parmigiano, shaved

Dressing

1 clove roasted garlic, crushed

2–3 anchovies, drained and oil reserved

1 teaspoon Dijon mustard

100ml (3fl oz) extra virgin olive oil

1 lemon juice and zest

1 egg yolk

60g (2oz) grated parmesan

Sea salt and pepper

2 tablespoons chopped parsley

Toasted torn sourdough to serve

Cut fillet into four equal portions. Place each piece of beef between two pieces of baking paper and pound with a meat mallet or rolling pin until beef is the thickness of tissue paper. Remove top sheet of baking paper and tip serving plate onto meat. Trim edges of beef to fit the plate neatly. Re-cover with baking paper and refrigerate until required. Repeat with remaining meat.

To make the dressing, place garlic, anchovies and mustard and lemon juice into a bowl and mash together with a fork until smooth; add egg yolk and mix well. Using a whisk, slowly add oil in a steady stream while whisking continuously. Season to taste and stir through parmesan and parsley, cover and refrigerate until required.

To poach quail eggs, bring a medium saucepan of water to the simmer. Carefully drop whole eggs in their shells into pan and cook for 2 minutes. Remove immediately and place into a bowl of ice water to stop the cooking process. Stand 5 minutes or until completely cold. Drain well and return to bowl. Cover with enough white vinegar so that eggs are fully submerged. Stand for 7–10 minutes or until shell is easily removed. Drain eggs, peel and set aside. Quail eggs should be still soft and gooey in the centre.

To serve, remove baking paper from carpaccio and place onto serving plates; drizzle with a little of the reserved anchovy oil. Cut each lettuce quarter into 3 or 4 thin wedges and place onto beef. Scatter over capers and place an egg onto each plate. Drizzle over dressing and garnish with shaved parmesan.

Break the soft egg just before serving. Serve with torn pieces of toasted sourdough (pictured left on the following page).

WINTER BEEF CARPACCIO WITH ROASTED BLACK PEPPER OIL AND SCORCHED ONIONS

SERVES 4

Preheat oven to 200°C (390°F) and place onions into a baking dish; drizzle with olive oil and season with salt and pepper. Bake, turning onions every ten minutes, for 40 minutes or until onions are dark golden and softened but not collapsed.

Cut fillet into four equal portions. Place each piece of beef between two pieces of baking paper and pound with a meat mallet or rolling pin until beef is the thickness of tissue paper. Remove top sheet of baking paper and tip serving plate onto meat. Trim edges of beef to fit the plate neatly. Re-cover with baking paper and refrigerate until required. Repeat with remaining meat.

Cut mushrooms into 1cm (½in) thick slices through the stalk. Heat oil in a frying pan and add mushrooms and garlic; cook for 4–5 minutes. Season to taste with salt and pepper, and remove and cool.

To serve, remove baking paper from beef, drizzle with a little of the black pepper oil and a pinch of sea salt. Top with scorched onion and cooked mushrooms.

Crumble over feta and garnish with baby watercress. Serve immediately with grissini. (pictured right on the following page).

200g (7oz) piece beef fillet, trimmed and denuded

4 large field mushrooms, peeled

50ml (1¾ fl oz) olive oil

1 clove garlic, finely sliced

150g (5oz) Persian feta cheese

1 punnet baby watercress for garnish

1 quantity of roasted black pepper oil (see Basics)

Scorched onions

16 small pickling onions, peeled and left whole

50ml olive oil

Sea salt and pepper

Grissini to serve

SHAVED SERRANO HAM, GRATED OX HEART TOMATO, AND OLIVE OIL BREAD

SERVES 4

300g (10½oz) finely shaved Serrano white leg air-dried ham or prosciutto

Olive oil bread

2 teaspoons dried yeast

1 teaspoon caster sugar

60ml (2fl oz) olive oil

300g (10½oz) plain flour, plus extra for kneading

20g (⅔oz) sea salt flakes

2 tablespoons rosemary sprigs

1 large ripe ox heart tomato

1 tablespoon extra virgin olive oil

Sea salt and pepper

Pitted black olives to serve

Combine 200ml (7fl oz) warm water, yeast, sugar and 40ml of oil in a bowl and mix well. Stand for 5 minutes or until mixture is frothy.

Mix flour and sea salt in a large mixing bowl and make a well in the centre; pour in yeast mixture and stir with a wooden spoon until well combined. Using clean hands, bring the dough together and tip onto a floured work surface. Knead for 10 minutes or until smooth and elastic. Rub dough ball with a little olive oil and return to mixing bowl. Cover with a tea towel or plastic wrap and stand in a warm place for 30–45 minutes or until doubled in size.

Preheat oven to 200°C (400°F) and grease a 20cm x 30cm (8in x 12in) baking tray. Knock down dough with fist and turn out onto a lightly floured work surface; knead for 2 minutes. Press into prepared pan, cover and prove for another 30 minutes.

Using your fingers, press dimples into the dough evenly. Brush with remaining oil, sprinkle with salt and rosemary and bake for 25–30 minutes or until bread is golden and sounds hollow when the base is tapped. Cool on a wire rack.

Grate tomato on the large setting of a box grater and collect flesh and juices in a bowl. Stir in oil and season well with salt and pepper.

To serve, cut olive oil bread into thin 12cm (5in) long strips and place onto the side of each plate. Place a small bowl of grated tomato into the centre and place ham alongside the bread. Scatter over black olives and serve.

SWEET RED SALAD

SERVES 4

Preheat oven to 180°C (350°F) and place beetroot onto tray, drizzle over vinegar and season with salt and pepper. Cover dish with foil and bake for 45 minutes or until beetroot is cooked. Remove and cool, reserve any remaining pan juices.

At the same time, place shallots into a small baking dish and drizzle with oil, toss to coat and roast alongside beetroot for 20-30 minutes or until golden and soft.

Heat sugar in a small saucepan until melted, stir in reserved beetroot juices and simmer until dissolved. Add walnuts and toss to coat. Place onto a lined baking tray and roast in oven for 5-10 minutes or until toasted. Remove and set aside.

To make the dressing, whisk vinegars, oil and lemon zest together until well combined; season to taste.

Cut brick pastry into four 5cm (2in) wide and 20cm (8in) long strips and wrap around a greased 12cm (5in) ring mould. Bake in hot oven for 5 minutes or until crisp. Remove from mould and place onto serving plates.

Combine roasted beetroot, shallots and walnuts and drizzle over with half the dressing; toss gently to mix. Spoon vegetables into the centre of pastry ring, making sure that each serve has an equal portion of vegetables. Top with a dollop of sheep's yoghurt and garnish with micro herbs. Just before serving, drizzle any remaining dressing around the outside of the plate and serve.

200g (7oz) golden beetroot, peeled and cut in halved

200g (7oz) baby red beetroot, peeled and trimmed

3 tablespoons (40ml) sherry vinegar

Sea salt and pepper

12 Asian shallots, peeled and trimmed

2 tablespoons (30ml) olive oil

2 teaspoons white sugar

90g walnut halves

150ml (5 fl oz) sheep's milk yoghurt

2 sheets Tunisian brick pastry

Dressing

25ml sherry vinegar

1½ tablespoons (20ml) Pedro Ximénez sherry

100ml (3½fl oz) extra virgin olive oil

Zest of a lemon

Micro herbs to garnish

TRUFFLE HONEY AND PARSNIP SOUP

SERVES 4-6

1.5kg (3lb) young parsnips, peeled, trimmed and halved

3 cloves garlic, sliced

2 sprigs thyme, plus extra for garnish

60ml (2fl oz) truffled honey

60ml (2fl oz) extra virgin olive oil

Sea salt and pepper

1 onion, finely chopped

1 leek, white part only, finely sliced

1.5 litres (48fl oz) chicken stock

125ml (4½fl oz) cream

1 parsnip, peeled and very thinly sliced

Preheat oven to 180°C (350°F) and place parsnips into a large roasting dish. Scatter over garlic and thyme. Drizzle over honey and 40ml of olive oil. Season well with salt and pepper and toss to coat evenly. Roast parsnips in oven for 30-40 minutes, turning parsnips over half way, until they are caramelised and softened.

Heat remaining oil in a large deep saucepan over medium heat and cook onion and leek for 5 minutes or until softened, but not coloured. Add roasted parsnips, juices, all herbs and garlic and continue cooking for a further 2-3 minutes. Pour in stock and increase heat to high; bring to the boil. Reduce heat to medium and simmer for a further 30 minutes.

Using a stick blender, process soup until smooth and strain through a fine sieve; return to pan and reheat until hot. Stir in cream and season to taste with salt and pepper.

Deep fry the thinly sliced parsnip to make crisps for garnish

Divide soup among soup bowls and sprinkle with thyme, a little olive oil and extra black pepper and some of the parsnip crisps.

ASPARAGUS SALAD PISSLADIERE WITH GRAPE FONDUE

SERVES 6

Heat oil in a deep saucepan over medium heat and add onion. Cook, stirring occasionally, for 10-12 minutes or until caramelised and softened. Stir in sugar, wine and seasoning, and simmer for 45 minutes or until thick and of a jam-like consistency. Remove from heat and cool completely.

Preheat oven to 180°C (350°F) and line a baking tray with baking paper. Place one sheet of pastry onto prepared tray and spread half the onion jam over the pastry; place second sheet over the top. Press down firmly and prick surface evenly with a fork. Cover stack with a metal baking tray and bake for 10-12 minutes or until pastry is cooked through; remove and cool.

Reduce grape juice in a small saucepan over medium/high heat until reduced by half; add cream and simmer for a further 5 minutes or until reduced by a quarter. Whisk through diced cold butter to form a thick sauce. Take care not to boil sauce. Season with salt and pepper.

Cut pastry into 20 x 1cm (½in) wide strips and return to baking tray. Top each pastry strip with remaining onion jam and taleggio cheese. Warm in oven just before serving.

Place 2 strips of pastry onto each serving plate, allowing a gap down the middle. Toss asparagus, grapes, frisée and rocket together and scatter over the centre of each plate. Drizzle with the grape fondue and serve.

Onion jam

50ml (1¾fl oz) olive oil

1kg (2lb) brown onions, chopped

200g (7oz) brown sugar

150ml (5¼fl oz) white wine

Sea salt and pepper

Pissladiere

2 sheets butter puff pastry

100g (3½oz) tallegio washed rind cheese, sliced

2 bunches baby asparagus, trimmed and blanched

400g (13oz) small seedless grapes

50g (1½oz) baby rocket leaves, trimmed

1 punnet small frisée lettuce leaves

Grape fondue

150ml (5fl oz) fresh grape juice

100ml (3½fl oz) cream

90g (3oz) cold butter, diced

Squeeze lemon juice

PETUNA COLD-SMOKED OCEAN TROUT SERVED WITH WARM FENNEL BROTH

SERVES 4

Fennel broth

50g (1½oz) butter

2 heads of fennel, finely sliced

1 onion, finely sliced

½ clove garlic, crushed

100ml (3½fl oz) white wine

200ml (7fl oz) vegetable stock

100ml (3½fl oz) cream

60ml (2fl oz) white Sambucca

240g (8oz) smoked ocean trout, trimmed and cut into 1cm (½in) dice

½ quantity of roasted black pepper oil (see Basics)

60g (2oz) ocean trout roe

1 slice brioche bread, cut into small croutons and toasted

80g (3oz) fennel, sliced thinly

½ bunch fennel tips

Melt butter in a large saucepan over medium heat and add fennel, onion and garlic. Cook, stirring for 3–5 minutes, until softened but not coloured. Stir in wine and reduce by half. Add vegetable stock, reduce heat and simmer for 20 minutes. Add cream and season with salt and pepper. Add Sambucca and blend soup until smooth.

Combine diced ocean trout with roasted black pepper oil and ocean trout roe. Add croutons and fennel and mix gently.

To serve, place ocean trout mixture into a serving glass or dish; garnish with fennel tips and serve the warm fennel broth on the side, to be poured over at the table.

An alternate way to serve this dish is in a wide-rimmed soup bowl or martini glass.

TAPAS

Tapas have evolved over time, and are no longer leftovers with a spicy tomato sauce on the top! If you want to feel good about your cooking ability, prepare some tapas and present them in small bowls next to each other. This is a great alternative for an entrée. Use your imagination or walk around a fruit market and deli to get some ideas and create a menu of your own.

GOAT'S CHEESE AND BLOOD ORANGE DIP WITH SWEET POTATO CHIPS

SERVES 4

300ml (10fl oz) cream

Pinch cayenne pepper

Pinch sea salt

150g (5oz) goat's cheese

10ml (1 dessertspoon) blood orange juice

50ml (1¾fl oz) lemon juice

30g (1oz) caster sugar

1 medium-sized sweet potato

Oil

Sea salt

In a bowl, lightly whisk the cream until thick; season with cayenne and sea salt. Stir in goat's cheese and whisk to a thick cream.

Meanwhile, simmer the orange and lemon juice with the sugar until thick and reduced. Allow to cool.

To make the sweet potato chips: using a potato peeler, slice sweet potato into thin slices. Deep fry in hot oil until crisp and golden. Drain on a paper towel and season with salt.

To serve, place the dip into a bowl and drizzle over the blood orange juice. Serve with sweet potato chips.

TUNA, JAMÓN AND TOMATO

SERVES 4

1 Roma tomato

Sea salt and pepper

1 medium red chilli, finely diced

60ml (2fl oz) extra virgin olive oil

Fresh red basil leaves

4 x 20g (⅔oz) slices fresh tuna

4 slices of shaved Serrano ham

Peel and deseed the tomato, cut into 1cm (½in) dice and place into a bowl. Season with salt and pepper, add red chilli, olive oil and basil leaves.

Wrap the tuna in a slice of ham. Stand upright on the serving plate and spoon the dressing over.

SEARED SCALLOPS WITH RADISH AND VEGETABLE SALAD

SERVES 4

Heat olive oil in a frying pan over medium/high heat and sear the scallops for 1 minute each side.

Mix the shredded apple, radish and carrot with the coriander then place on the top of the warm scallops. Garnish with salmon roe.

2 tablespoons olive oil

4 Hervey Bay or half shell scallops

1 pink lady apple, finely shredded

3 red radishes, finely shredded

1 small carrot, finely shredded

Fresh baby coriander leaves

30g (1oz) salmon roe

South

FRIED OYSTERS

SERVES 4

3 egg whites

60g (2oz) rice flour

Sea salt and pepper

8 Pacific oysters

500ml (16fl oz) vegetable oil

Dusting of sumac spice

Lemon wedges, to garnish

Lightly whisk egg whites to soft peaks. Combine rice flour with salt and pepper and then dip oyster meat into the flour. Shake off excess and coat in the egg whites.

Deep fry oysters in hot oil for 30 seconds; remove and drain onto absorbent paper. Dust with sumac spice and place back into warm oyster shells. Serve immediately with lemon wedge

MOZZARELLA, BEETROOT AND HORSERADISH

SERVES 4

Rub the beetroot with half the olive oil and bake in a moderate oven (180°C (350°F)) for 1 hour or until tender. Cool slightly, peel and grate on a cheese grater.

Mix the grated beetroot with the horseradish, add a little orange zest, vinegar and remaining oil; adjust seasoning to taste.

To serve, drain the mozzarella for 15 minutes, rip in half and place on serving plate. Spoon the beetroot sauce over and finish with the remaining orange zest.

2 medium beetroots

60ml (2fl oz) olive oil

1 piece of fresh horseradish, grated

1 orange, zested

Sea salt and pepper

Splash cabernet vinegar

2 pieces fresh mozzarella

MAINS

All of these recipes are my favourites, and are achievable in the home. Each of the more complex dishes are followed by an easier option, using the same primary ingredients and flavours. I suggest you try the simpler recipes first, building up to restaurant standard as you gain more confidence.

Professionally we break these meals down into components and so should you. Don't try to cook everything at once. Planning and timing play a big part; try to select dishes that are seasonal and within your skill level. When you are cooking the main course there is a fair chance that you have had a drink and that the kitchen is now covered in dirty dishes, so space is at a premium!

Remember, when entertaining, the chef is also a guest!

SNAPPER PUTTANESCA WITH ROASTED GARLIC AIOLI

SERVES 6

This is one of my favourites. I've also included another snapper dish that celebrates great flavours on the following page.

Preheat oven to 180°C (350°F).

To make the roasted garlic aioli, wrap garlic in foil and roast for 25 minutes or until garlic is tender. Cool slightly and squeeze out flesh. Mash with a fork until smooth and spoon into the bowl of a food processor. Add to mayonnaise and mix well.

Meanwhile, slice eggplants into 2cm (¾in) thick rounds. Place in a colander and sprinkle liberally with fine salt. Set aside for 15 minutes. Rinse eggplant thoroughly and pat dry. Pan fry eggplant slices in hot oil for 1–2 minutes each side, or until golden. Transfer to a roasting tray and bake in oven until tender. Keep warm.

To make herb oil, process herbs with oil until smooth; strain through fine sieve and set aside.

Place tomatoes onto a lined flat baking tray and season with salt and pepper. Roast in preheated oven for 45 minutes, until soft and concentrated. Cool and chop coarsely. Heat 1 tablespoon of oil in a large frying pan and add anchovies, olives, shallots and chilli, cook for 2–3 minutes. Stir in chopped roasted tomatoes and mix well. Reduce heat and simmer until sauce is very thick. Adjust seasoning to taste.

Season snapper fillets with salt and pepper. Pan fry, skin side down, until crisp. Turn and cook for a further minute.

To serve, place a piece of eggplant in the centre of each plate. Top with fish and spoon tomato sauce over the top. Drizzle some herb oil around the plate. Finish with a slice of lemon and roasted garlic aioli.

Roasted garlic aioli
1 garlic bulb

1 quantity of mayonnaise (see Basics)

2 large eggplants (aubergines)

Fine cooking salt

100ml olive oil

Herb oil
½ bunch fresh chives

½ bunch flat parsley leaves

100ml (3½fl oz) extra virgin olive oil

6 ripe Roma tomatoes, halved lengthways

Sea salt and freshly ground black pepper

80ml (3oz) olive oil

4 anchovies, chopped

100g (3½oz) black olives, sliced

2 French shallots, finely chopped

2 small red chillies, thinly sliced

6 x 200g (7oz) snapper fillets, skin on

1 lemon, sliced

PANFRIED SNAPPER FILLETS WITH LEMON BUTTER

SERVES 6

If you love these flavours, once you have mastered this dish, try the recipe on the previous page.

6 x 200g (7oz) snapper fillets, skin on

Sea salt and pepper

Zest of 1 lemon

3 tablespoons extra virgin olive oil

Lemon butter sauce

150g (5oz) unsalted butter

100ml (3½fl oz) cream

Zest and juice of 1 lemon

½ bunch fresh chives, chopped

Potato mash to serve (see Sides)

Score snapper skin and rub with salt and lemon zest. Heat oil and cook snapper for 2–3 minutes. Remove and keep warm.

Add cream to a small saucepan, bring to the boil and simmer for a few minutes to reduce. As cream begins to thicken, remove from heat and whisk in the cold butter. Add lemon juice and zest, stir in chopped chives, season to taste.

Serve snapper with potato mash and drizzle over lemon butter sauce.

NAKED SHELLFISH RAVIOLI WITH SQUID BOLOGNESE

SERVES 4-6

Capsicum (pepper) sauce

1½ tablespoons extra virgin olive oil

2 cloves garlic, crushed

1 red capsicum (pepper), seeds and membrane removed, and diced

1 long red chilli, chopped

Herb pangrattato

2 thick slices sourdough bread, crust removed and diced

3 tablespoons olive oil

1 clove garlic, crushed

Zest of 1 lemon

Sprig lemon thyme

Chopped parsley

Naked ravioli

300g (10½oz) medium green prawns, peeled and deveined

130g (1oz) raw bug meat, chopped

130g (1oz) raw lobster tail, chopped

2 large eggs, whites only

200ml (10fl oz) cream

Sea salt to taste

100g (3½oz) cooked crab meat, plus extra for garnish

1 litre (32fl oz) vegetable stock or water

Bolognese sauce

1kg (2lb) cleaned Hawkesbury River squid

3 tablespoons extra virgin olive oil

1 onion, finely diced

1 clove garlic, crushed

1 leek, white part only, finely diced

1 stick celery, finely diced

1 small carrot, peeled and finely diced

1 teaspoon tomato paste

375ml (12fl oz) red wine

1 teaspoon sugar

1 stick cinnamon

2 cloves, wrapped in muslin bag

250ml (9fl oz) capsicum coulis

500ml (¾pint) crushed tomato passata

Sea salt to taste

For the capsicum sauce, heat oil and garlic together in a small saucepan over medium heat until garlic is fragrant. Stir in remaining ingredients. Reduce heat, cover and simmer for 30 minutes or until capsicum has softened and collapsed. Remove from heat and process or blend until smooth. Pass through a fine sieve and set aside.

To make the pangrattato, process bread in a food processor to form coarse breadcrumbs. Heat oil in a large frying pan and add breadcrumbs and remaining ingredients. Toast, stirring continuously, until bread is golden and crisp. Remove and drain on kitchen paper.

For the bolognese, place squid into the bowl of a food processor and pulse until finely minced. Heat oil in a deep pan over medium/high heat and cook onion and garlic until softened and fragrant. Add squid mince and cook for 2 minutes. Add leek, celery, carrot and tomato paste and continue cooking for a further 10 minutes, until softened but not coloured. Stir in wine, sugar, cinnamon and cloves and simmer for 5 minutes. Add reserved capsicum coulis and passata. Half cover with a lid and simmer for 1 hour.

To make the ravioli, place all seafood into the chilled base of a food processor and pulse 3–4 times or until finely chopped. Add egg whites and pulse a few more times, or until incorporated. Mixture should resemble a tight ball at this point. Add cream and pulse for 30 seconds. Stir in the cooked crab and place the mousse in a fridge for 30 minutes to set.

Bring a shallow pan of vegetable stock or water to the boil; reduce heat to a simmer. Using 2 tablespoons, form small balls of mousse and drop into the hot liquid. Poach for 2–3 minutes.

To serve, divide bolognese into serving bowls. Top with 3 ravioli and garnish with extra cooked flaked crab meat. Sprinkle with pangrattato and serve immediately.

ANGEL HAIR SHELLFISH PASTA

SERVES 6

This is one of my favourite seafood pasta dishes. It's quick and easy and delicious!

Bring a large pan of salted water to the boil and cook pasta until al dente; drain.

Cook garlic in oil over medium heat for a few minutes. Add prawns and scallops cook for 2 minutes. Toss warm seafood and oil through pasta. Add crab meat and parsley and season with salt and pepper. Serve topped with sliced chilli.

500g (1lb 2 oz) angel hair pasta

60ml (2fl oz) extra virgin olive oil

1 clove garlic, finely sliced

12 medium green prawns, peeled

12 fresh scallops

100g (3½oz) cooked picked crab meat

Juices of 1 lemon and 1 lime

1 punnet baby parsley

Sea salt and pepper

1 long red chilli, finely sliced

SEARED PRAWN, PUMPKIN AND SPINACH ROTOLO

SERVES 4–6

This is one of my signature dishes. When I don't have time, the combination of flavours works just as well in the less-structured recipe on the following page.

500g (1lb) pumpkin, peeled and diced

2 cloves garlic, chopped

Pinch nutmeg

60g (2oz) butter

Sea salt and pepper

60g (2oz) mustard fruits, chopped

100g (3½oz) baby spinach

4 French shallots, finely chopped

500g (1lb) large fresh pasta sheets, rolled thinly (see Basics)

300g (10½oz) full cream ricotta, drained

1 egg, beaten

100g (3½oz) fresh breadcrumbs

60g (2oz) freshly grated parmesan

3 tablespoons olive oil

60g (2oz) butter

12 medium green prawns, peeled and deveined with tails intact

Nut butter

90g (3oz) cold butter

30g (1oz) pumpkin seeds

½ bunch fresh sage

Lemon wedges, to serve

Preheat oven to 180°C (350°F) and place pumpkin, garlic, nutmeg and half the butter into a large baking dish. Season with salt and pepper and roast for 30 minutes until soft and golden. Process roasted pumpkin with mustard fruits in a food processor until smooth. Pass through a fine sieve and heat in a small saucepan over medium heat, until thick and dry. Remove and cool completely.

Melt remaining butter in a large pan and cook shallots for 2–3 minutes. Add spinach and cook for a further minute, or until spinach has wilted. Cool slightly.

Place fresh pasta sheets onto a clean tea towel or napkin and spread some of the pumpkin purée all over. Scatter over a little of the spinach mixture and crumble over ricotta. Roll up pasta in the tea towel to form a neat roll. Take care to seal the ends and sides by tying the ends of the tea towel together with some twine. Drop into boiling water for 5 minutes, remove and allow to cool completely in the fridge.

When cold, unwrap the rotolo from tea towel and slice into 5cm (2in) thick pieces. Brush each slice with egg and dust with breadcrumbs and parmesan. Pan fry in a little oil and butter for a few minutes on each side, until golden and crisp. Remove and place onto serving plates. Using the same pan, add a little butter and cook the prawns for 2 minutes, then place on top of the rotolo.

In another pan, melt the cold butter over high heat and cook quickly until it has a nutty smell. Add the pumpkin seeds and sage and a squeeze of lemon. Spoon the butter over the prawns and rotolo. Serve with lemon wedges.

SPICE-ROASTED PUMPKIN WITH RICOTTA AND SAGE NUT BUTTER PRAWNS

SERVES 6

I love these flavours so much, when I don't have time, I use this quick recipe.

Preheat oven to 200°C (400°F).

Cut pumpkin into large pieces and coat with harissa, ground cumin and half of the olive oil. Place into a roasting dish and season. Roast in oven for 30 minutes until caramelised and tender.

Heat remaining oil in a frying pan, cook prawns for 2–3 minutes and remove. Add butter to the same pan and cook until it has a nutty smell. Stir in seeds, sage and a squeeze of lemon juice. Return prawns to pan and keep warm.

Serve roasted pumpkin topped with a spoon of ricotta. Spoon over prawns and sage nut butter.

1kg (2lb) pumpkin, skin on
(I prefer the Kent variety)

1 tablespoon harissa paste

1 tablespoon ground cumin

60ml (2fl oz) extra virgin olive oil

Sea salt and pepper

12 medium green prawns, peeled

90g (3oz) salted butter

30g (1oz) pumpkin seeds

½ bunch fresh sage leaves

1 lemon

150g (5oz) fresh ricotta cheese

¼ bunch coriander, leaves picked

TWICE-COOKED PORK BELLY WITH ROASTED APPLE MARMALADE

SERVES 6

This is the most requested dish in my restaurant. It took three months to perfect, so be prepared for a challenge. On the next page, I've included a recipe with similar stunning flavours, with a much simpler method.

1.5kg (3lb) pork belly, rib removed and skin on

100g (3½oz) sea salt

3 teaspoons Chinese five spice

Apple marmalade

3 pink lady apples, peeled, cored and cut into wedges

150g (5oz) butter, melted

1 vanilla bean, split lengthways and seeds scraped

100g (3½oz) caster sugar

Grated apple and caramelised balsamic, to serve

Preheat oven to 190°C (375°F).

To make the apple marmalade, place apple into a small bowl and pour over butter and vanilla seeds. Sprinkle sugar over and toss apples to coat evenly. Place onto a lined baking tray and cook in oven for 20 minutes until soft and caramelised. Cool and set aside.

Place pork, skin side down, onto a chopping board. With a sharp knife, stab pork flesh evenly about 15 times. Mix salt and five spice powder together and rub over pork belly. Cover and refrigerate overnight.

Preheat oven to 140°C (275°F) and place pork belly, flesh side down, onto a baking tray. Bake for 45 minutes. Remove pork from oven, drain surplus liquid and transfer to a heavy metal roasting tray lined with silicon paper, skin side down.

Increase oven temperature to 180°C (350°F). Place a second sheet of baking paper over the top of the pork belly, followed by a sheet of cardboard. Weigh down with a heavy ovenproof pan or dish and return to oven for 35–40 minutes.

Remove from oven and discard weights, cardboard and baking paper. Turn pork belly over so that crackling is now on the top. Cut pork belly into six 15cm (6in) portions. Remove crackling by sliding a small knife between fat and skin.

To serve, reheat pork belly in a medium oven without the crackling. Place some apple marmalade on the pork then place the crackling back on the top.

Serve with some grated fresh apple, apple marmalade and caramelised balsamic vinegar brushed on the plate.

CRISPY PORK BELLY WITH BAKED STUFFED APPLES

SERVES 6

Preheat oven to 160°C (325°F).

Score belly skin and rub in salt and pepper evenly. Place onto a wire rack in a roasting dish, skin side up, and bake for 1½ hours.

Core the apples. Combine remaining ingredients and spoon into core centre of each apple. Bake in oven with pork for 1 hour.

Remove apples and turn the pork over. Increase oven temperature to 200°C (400°F) and roast for a further 30 minutes.

Serve pork slices with stuffed baked apples, either whole or halved, and drizzle with pan juices from the roasting tray.

1.2kg (2lb 6½oz) pork belly

1 tablespoon sea salt

2 teaspoons ground black pepper

6 large green apples

100g (3½oz) dates, finely chopped

50g (1½oz) roasted almonds, chopped

50g (1½oz) raisins

2 tablespoons brown sugar

Pinch ground cinnamon

100g (3½oz) butter

4 butterflied spatchcock

2 lemons, sliced

2 cloves garlic, sliced

Sea salt and pepper

Olive oil to cover

Lemon-mint yoghurt

1 slice of preserved lemon, washed and
finely chopped

1 tablespoon chopped mint

100ml (3½fl oz) sheep's milk yoghurt
(or thick Greek yoghurt)

1½ tablespoons olive oil

Tomato harissa

2 teaspoons harissa or to taste

1½ tablespoons olive oil

150g (5oz) roasted tomato jam (see
Basics)

Za'atar dressing

1½ tablespoons lemon juice

60ml (2fl oz) extra virgin olive oil

1 tablespoon za'atar spices, dry
roasted

Israeli cous cous salad

120g (4oz) Israeli cous cous

60ml (2fl oz) olive oil

1 red onion, finely chopped

2 teaspoons cumin, ground

1 teaspoon coriander, ground

2 tomatoes, chopped

20g (⅔oz) sultanas

½ bunch fresh coriander, leaves chopped

50g (1½oz) slivered almonds or
pistachio nuts

LEMON-SPICED SPATCHCOCK WITH ISRAELI COUS COUS

SERVES 4

Preheat oven to 180°C (350°F).

Using fingers, ease skin away from breast meat on each spatchcock. Slide in slices of lemon and 2 slices of garlic. Season with salt and pepper and lay into the base of a large roasting dish. Scatter over remaining lemon slices and garlic cloves. Pour over enough olive oil to cover spatchcock completely; cook for 45 minutes.

Remove spatchcock from oil and cut drumsticks off. Set aside.

Combine lemon-mint yoghurt ingredients and refrigerate. Set aside.

Mix tomato harissa together and set aside.

Whisk lemon juice, oil and za'atar spices together and season to taste. Set aside.

Make the Israeli cous cous salad. Cook cous cous in a saucepan of boiling water until swollen and soft. Drain and refresh with cold water.

Heat oil in a pan and cook onion until softened. Add spices and chopped tomatoes and cook a further 5–8 minutes or until tomatoes have broken down. Stir in remaining ingredients and cooked cous cous and warm through. Stir in half the lemon mint yoghurt, and coriander leaves.

Place spatchcock drumsticks into a small frying pan and cook until skin is crisp. Pan fry the breast until golden and crisp.

To serve, spoon the cous cous salad onto plates, top with roasted drumsticks and breast. Dot remaining yoghurt and tomato harissa alternately around plate, and finally drizzle over za'atar dressing.

SIMPLE LEMON CHICKEN WITH MINT YOGHURT

SERVES 6

A simpler Middle Eastern take on the Lemon-spiced Spatchcock recipe on the previous page.

Preheat oven to 180°C (350°F).

Using fingers, ease skin away from breast meat and slide in lemon and garlic slices. Place spatchcock and potatoes into a deep large baking dish and season well. Pour over enough oil to cover completely and bake for 45 minutes.

Drain spatchcock and potatoes. Pan fry spatchcock and potatoes in a hot frying pan until crisp and golden. Add lemon halves to pan for a few minutes to caramelise.

Combine lemon yoghurt, season and mix well.

Carve spatchcock and serve drizzled with lemon yoghurt and caramelised lemons on top.

4 spatchcock, butterflied

2 lemons, sliced

2 cloves garlic, sliced

Sea salt and pepper

1kg (2lb) small kipfler potatoes, scrubbed

Olive oil to cover

3 lemons, halved

Lemon mint yoghurt

1 slice preserved lemon, washed and chopped

1 tablespoon chopped mint

100ml (3½fl oz) sheep's milk yoghurt or thick Greek yoghurt

1 tablespoon olive oil

SLOW-COOKED LAMB TORTELLI WITH POACHED AND ROASTED CHERRIES, CHERRY TOFFEE

SERVES 4-6

800g (1½lb) lamb shoulder

3 cloves garlic, crushed

1 lemon, sliced

2-3 sprigs fresh rosemary

Sea salt and pepper

3 tablespoons extra virgin olive oil

3 French shallots, finely chopped

100ml (3½fl oz) red wine

500ml (17fl oz) beef stock

4 x 4-bone lamb racks

Cherry toffee

300ml (10fl oz) red wine

2 tablespoons caster sugar

1 teaspoon ground cinnamon

Pinch ground ginger

Pinch ground nutmeg

1kg (2lb) fresh cherries, with stone removed

90g (1½oz) brown sugar

60ml (2fl oz) balsamic vinegar

1 quantity of pasta dough (see Basics)

Preheat oven to 160°C (325°F) and place lamb shoulder into a baking dish. Sprinkle with 2 cloves garlic, lemon, rosemary, salt and pepper and half the oil. Cover with foil and roast for 45 minutes. Remove foil and continue cooking for a further 15 minutes. Remove from oven and cool completely before slicing or pulling meat apart.

Heat remaining oil in a large pan over medium heat and cook shallots and garlic for 3-4 minutes. Add cooked lamb, wine and stock and simmer for 30 minutes or until thick and liquid has evaporated. Adjust seasoning and cool completely. This is the tortelli filling.

Roll pasta dough out thinly. Place spoonfuls of lamb mix along the pasta, brush around the edges with a little water then lay another sheet of pasta over the top. Cut into circles then shape into tortelli by using your little finger to indent one side. Cook in a pot of boiling salted water until tender.

In a saucepan, warm the wine, caster sugar and spices, simmer for 3 minutes then add the cherries. Bring back to the simmer and remove from the heat and allow to cool in the syrup.

To make the cherry toffee, place 6 cherries into a small saucepan. Add brown sugar and balsamic vinegar and simmer gently for 10 minutes, stirring occasionally. Strain liquid into a small serving jug, return to the saucepan and reduce to a toffee-like syrup consistency.

Season the lamb rack and roast in a medium (180°C (350°F)) oven for 14 minutes until pink. Allow to rest and slice into cutlets.

Remove the cherries from the syrup and roast in a hot oven for 10 minutes.

To serve, place tortelli with cherries down the centre of each plate. Arrange cutlets neatly and drizzle the glaze down either side of plate.

SLOW-COOKED WARM LAMB SHOULDER SALAD

SERVES 6

If you love slow-cooked lamb as much as I do, you will find this recipe a little easier than the one on the previous page. It uses the same preparation for the lamb.

Preheat oven to 160°C (325°F).

Rub lamb with garlic, rosemary and one lemon slice. Place into a roasting dish. Season well and drizzle over 40ml of oil. Roast in oven for 1 hour. Remove and allow to cool, then slice thinly.

Combine spinach and mint on a large serving platter and scatter over sliced lamb. Top with crumbled feta and olives.

Whisk juice of remaining lemon and olive oil together and season. Add 1–2 tablespoons of any pan juices and mix well. Pour over salad and serve with grilled flat bread.

800g (1½lb) lamb shoulder

3 cloves garlic, crushed

1 stalk fresh rosemary, leaves picked

2 lemons

Sea salt and pepper

80ml (3fl oz) extra virgin olive oil

100g (3½oz) baby spinach leaves

1 bunch mint, leaves picked

150g (5oz) Greek feta, crumbled

150g (5oz) Kalamata olives

Grilled flat bread to serve

BRAISED BEEF CHEEKS WITH STOCK POT CARROTS

SERVES 4-6

1.5kg (3lb) beef cheeks

1 x 750ml (24fl oz) bottle shiraz

4 sprigs thyme, leaves picked

2 cloves garlic, chopped

3 juniper berries

1 bay leaf

5 whole black peppercorns

100g (3½oz) plain flour

80ml (3oz) olive oil

1 litre (32fl oz) beef stock

1 onion, chopped

1 leek, sliced

Sea salt and pepper

1kg (2lb) medium whole carrots, peeled and left whole

Mashed potato (see Side Orders)

Marinate beef cheeks with half the wine, thyme, garlic and spices. Toss to coat evenly, cover and marinate overnight.

Drain cheeks and dust lightly in flour. Heat 2 tablespoons of oil in a heavy cast iron enamelled casserole dish and pan fry cheeks for 2–3 minutes. Set aside.

Into the pan, pour in remaining wine and stock, onion and leek and then return cheeks to pan. Add the whole carrots, cover and simmer over a low heat for 2 hours.

Carefully remove the carrots and slice lengthways. Set aside.

Return sauce to stove and continue simmering for a further 30 minutes, or until sauce is thick. Season to taste.

Preheat oven to 160°C (325°F) and place cheeks in baking dish. Spoon some of sauce over the cheeks. Reheat for 30 minutes, spooning sauce over to form a dark glaze.

To serve, place beef cheeks onto a serving of mashed potato then carefully lay the carrots on the top. Drizzle some sauce over.

GRILLED SIRLOIN ON THE BONE WITH SALT BRINE AND ROASTED MUSHROOM

SERVES 4

The salt brine helps to create a delicious crust to form on the steak.

Preheat oven 180°C (350°F).

Make salt brine by dissolving the rock salt into 250ml (9fl oz) of water.

Warm oil in a roasting dish in a preheated oven. Add bacon and garlic and cook for a few minutes, or until bacon is crisp and browned. Add butter and mushrooms, cup side up, and rosemary. Season with freshly ground black pepper, add beef stock and cook for 25 minutes, or until mushrooms are cooked. Strain any pan juices and reserve. Cover pan with foil and keep warm.

Place pan juices in a saucepan and reduce until concentrated and dark. Season to taste.

Heat a barbecue plate over high heat. Season steaks with pepper and brush the surface of each steak with salt brine. Sear on very hot plate for 1 minute. While steak is cooking, brush exposed side with brine. Turn steaks over and cook 1 minute. Repeat these steps 3 times, make sure you keep the heat high. The steaks will blacken and the centre will be rare. Allow to rest in a warm place for 10 minutes.

Serve steaks with roasted mushrooms and sauce.

60g (2½oz) rock salt

50ml (1¾fl oz) olive oil

8 rashers bacon

2 cloves garlic, sliced

30g (1oz) butter

600g (1lb 3½oz) small field mushrooms, trimmed

4 stalks fresh rosemary

Sea salt and pepper

100ml (3½fl oz) beef stock

4 x 400g (13oz) sirloin or beef ribs on the bone

PEPPERED VEAL RIBS WITH CELERIAC PURÉE

SERVES 4

Brine

100g (3½oz) rock sugar

60g (2oz) black peppercorns

30g (1oz) coriander seed

30g (1oz) Szechuan peppercorns

1 tablespoon chilli flakes

1 cinnamon stick

30g (1oz) allspice berries

4 star anise

1 tablespoon brown mustard seed

30g (1oz) whole cumin seed

1 bunch fresh coriander

150g (5oz) rock salt

1 x 2kg (4lb) veal rack with ribs on, tied by your butcher

3 tablespoons olive oil

Celeriac purée

1½ tablespoons olive oil

1 clove garlic, chopped

3 French shallots, chopped

100g (3½oz) arborio rice

250g (8oz) celeriac, peeled and diced

60ml (2fl oz) cream

500ml (16fl oz) milk

Sea salt and pepper

In a large pot or bucket mix all brine ingredients into 2.5 litres (5¼ pints) water, stir well and set aside. Add veal rack, cover and stand in the fridge for 2 hours. Remove and drain well.

Preheat oven to 200°C (400°F) and heat oil in a large frying pan. Season rib with freshly ground black pepper and seal in hot pan until golden. Transfer to a roasting pan and cook for 45 minutes. Allow to rest for 10 minutes before carving; keep warm.

To make the purée, heat oil in a pan over medium heat and gently cook garlic and shallots until softened. Add the rice and celeriac and cook for 2 minutes. Bring milk and cream to the boil then stir into the rice and celeriac; cover with buttered baking paper and a lid. Simmer for 12 minutes or until celeriac is tender and rice is cooked. Remove from heat and purée in a food processor until smooth. Season to taste.

Serve each guest a slice through the bone and a spoon of purée, sprinkled with celery leaves.

GRILLED VEAL CHOPS WITH RISOTTO

SERVES 6

Brush half the oil over veal chops and season with salt and pepper. Heat a grill plate over high heat and cook veal for 4 minutes on each side, or until cooked to your liking.

Heat remaining oil and half the butter in a heavy-based pan and add onion, garlic and celeriac. Stir for 3–4 minutes over medium heat, until softened but not coloured. Stir in rice and cook until the rice becomes transparent. Stir in a ladle of hot stock and stir over heat until stock is absorbed. Repeat, ladle by ladle, until all stock has been absorbed. Season to taste, and adjust risotto consistency with remaining stock so that it is loose and 'moves'. Stir in grated parmesan, cream and remaining butter.

Serve celeriac risotto with grilled veal chop and diced roasted celeriac.

Sprinkle with young celery leaves.

60ml (2fl oz) olive oil

6 large veal or pork chops

Sea salt and pepper

60g (2oz) butter

1 onion, chopped

2 cloves garlic, chopped

200g (7oz) bulb celeriac, peeled and grated

180g (6oz) arborio rice

600ml (12fl oz) hot chicken stock

Freshly grated parmesan

60ml (2fl oz) cream

Celeriac, diced and roasted

Young celery leaves

SPINACH AND MUSHROOM CROUSTADA

SERVES 4

3 sheets of good quality butter puff
pastry

Béchamel sauce

500ml (16fl oz) milk

1 small onion, studded with 3 cloves

1 bay leaf

1 clove garlic, peeled

40g (1½oz) butter

40g (1½oz) plain flour

Sea salt and freshly ground black
pepper

Pinch nutmeg

1 bunch English spinach, washed,
blanched and chopped

Mushroom purée

50g (1½oz) butter

2 French shallots, finely diced

2 cloves garlic, crushed

3 teaspoons fresh thyme leaves

500g (1lb) field mushrooms, chopped

Swiss brown mushrooms

400g (13oz) Swiss brown mushrooms,
trimmed and diced

50g (1½oz) butter

300g (10½oz) fontina cheese, diced

90g (3oz) grated parmesan

1 egg, beaten

Make the béchamel sauce by heating the milk in a large saucepan with studded onion, bay leaf and garlic over medium heat. Strain and set aside. Melt butter in the same pan and stir in flour. Mix until it forms a paste; cook for 1 minute without colouring. Gradually stir in hot milk, a little at a time and stir constantly, until mixture comes to the boil and thickens. Cook on a low simmer or in the oven for 45 minutes. Season with salt, pepper and nutmeg. Remove and allow to cool. Once béchamel is cold, stir through blanched, chopped spinach and set aside.

To make the purée, melt butter in a large frying pan over medium/high heat and add all ingredients. Stir for 10 minutes or until mushrooms have softened and all the liquid has evaporated. Season to taste and place into a strainer. Squeeze out any excess liquid and cool before processing to a smooth consistency.

Cook Swiss brown mushrooms in a pan with butter until softened. Season to taste and cool completely.

Preheat oven to 180°C (350°F) and line 2 baking trays with baking paper. Cut puff pastry into four 20cm x 12 cm (8in x 5in) rectangles. Spoon a line of spinach béchamel on the edge, followed by a line of purée. Top with cooked Swiss brown mushrooms, diced fontina cheese and parmesan and brush edges with beaten egg.

Fold over pastry to enclose and place onto baking trays. Brush with extra egg wash and bake for 20 minutes, or until pastry is golden and cooked through. Serve with your favourite vegetables on the side.

SIDES

Sides are a big feature on any menu; they allow people to satisfy their appetite and can give a more casual feel to any meal. At home, side meals are a great way of continuing to surprise your guests by adding more tasty, beautiful things to the table.

I love picking away at a salad or scooping up the last of the creamy mash.

I always make too much food when entertaining at home. I was recently told by a palm reader that it's a character trait and therefore not my fault!

CHIPS WITH ROSEMARY SALT

SERVES 4

Clever presentation can change the status of the simplest product.

1 stalk fresh rosemary, sprigs picked

60g (2oz) sea salt

1 litre (32fl oz) vegetable oil

500g (1lb) desiree or spunta potatoes

1 litre (32fl oz) cottonseed oil

Place rosemary and salt onto a baking tray and bake in a moderate oven (180°C (350°F)) for 10 minutes. Remove and cool completely. Grind in a mortar and pestle to a fine salt; set aside.

Heat the vegetable oil in a deep saucepan or wok to approx 180°C (350°F).

Peel and cut the potatoes into chips approx 7cm x 2cm (2¾in x ¾in). Rinse under cold water and dry thoroughly in a cloth. Cook in oil for 10 minutes, until soft but not coloured. Remove and drain onto kitchen paper. Allow chips to cool at this point, but do not place in a fridge.

Replace the vegetable oil with the cottonseed oil and heat to 200°C (400°F).

When ready to serve, place the chips into the hot cottonseed oil and cook for 5 minutes until crisp and golden. Remove and drain on kitchen paper. Serve sprinkled with rosemary salt.

For this presentation, fold textured grease-proof paper or stiff napkins into a tall glass.

MASHED POTATO WITH DOUBLE CREAM AND BUTTER

SERVES 4

Preheat a moderate oven to 180°C (350°F). Score the skins of the potatoes with a sharp knife. Lay them in a baking tray sprinkled with the rock salt and bake for 1½ hours, or until soft. While still hot, hold them in a tea towel and scoop the potato out of the skin. Press through a fine sieve or potato ricer.

Place mashed potato into a small saucepan and stir with a wooden spoon. Pour in cream and butter; adjust seasoning with salt and pepper and nutmeg.

Serve with a small knob of butter and some double cream poured over the top.

500g (1lb 2oz) desiree or scorpion potatoes

150g (5oz) rock salt

120ml (6fl oz) cream

125g (4½oz) unsalted butter, diced, plus extra for garnish

Salt and pepper

Pinch grated nutmeg

40ml (2fl oz) double cream

BROCCOLI WITH FRESH RED CHILLI

SERVES 4

Pinch sea salt

300g (10½oz) broccoli florets

60ml (2fl oz) good-quality olive oil

1 small red chill, finely sliced

1 clove garlic, chopped

Half fill a medium-sized saucepan with water and bring to the boil. Season with sea salt and add the broccoli, maintaining the boiling temperature.

Heat olive oil in a small frying pan over low heat and add garlic and red chilli; warm through gently without colouring the garlic.

Remove the broccoli from the water while still firm and bright green and drain. Add to frying pan and toss to coat.

Serve seasoned with sea salt.

GLAZED CARROT WITH CUMIN

SERVES 4

Toast the cumin seeds in a dry pan until fragrant; remove and set aside.

Combine sugar, water, butter and salt in a small frying pan and bring to the boil.

Slice carrots thinly on the diagonal, approximately 1cm (½in) thick. Add to pan and cook fast over high heat for approximately 8 minutes, or until carrots soften, and the liquid begins to evaporate; shake the pan gently as this happens. Coat the carrots in the buttery glaze.

To serve, spoon carrots onto plates and top with toasted cumin seeds.

Serve with green beans.

1 teaspoon cumin seeds

30g (1oz) caster sugar

250ml (9fl oz) mineral water

90g (3oz) unsalted butter

Pinch sea salt

500g (1lb) medium-sized carrots, peeled

GREEN BEANS WITH GARLIC, LEMON THYME AND SHALLOTS

SERVES 4

Pinch sea salt

300g (10½oz) good-quality green
beans, trimmed

60g (2oz) unsalted butter

1 clove garlic, crushed

2 French shallots, finely diced

1 sprig fresh lemon thyme

Sea salt and pepper

Bring a medium-sized pan of water to the boil and season with salt. Add beans and cook for 2–3 minutes.

Meanwhile, melt butter in a small frying pan and add garlic and shallots; cook until translucent.

Drain beans and add to the hot butter and shallots. Toss through picked thyme leaves and season to taste.

CRESS AND HERB SALAD WITH BOTRYTIS DRESSING

SERVES 4

Heat vegetable oil in a small frying pan over medium/high heat and fry the sliced shallots until crispy. Drain onto kitchen paper.

Combine olive oil and sauternes in a bowl and season with salt and pepper. Grate in a small amount of lemon zest and a small squeeze of lemon juice. Whisk to mix well.

Mix all of the washed cress and leaves in cold water, dry in a salad spinner and tip into a serving bowl. Dress the leaves with botrytis dressing and season to taste. Top with fried shallots and serve immediately.

100ml (3½fl oz) vegetable oil

2 French shallots, finely sliced

90ml (3fl oz) light olive oil

2 tablespoons (30ml) sauternes dessert wine (botrytis affected)

Sea salt and pepper

1 lemon

150g (5oz) upland cress

2 punnets baby coriander leaves

2 punnets baby red chard

1 bunch mizuna cress

2 punnets watercress

DESSERTS

This is a challenging part of the meal for me. First, I am diabetic, so desserts are off the menu, although I do sneak a taste as I go. I am one of the best bowl cleaners ever to work in a kitchen!

So many people have asked me why I love soufflé. I just do! So I've included several varieties to choose from.

RASPBERRY MERINGUE SOUFFLÉ

SERVES 6

Butter, for greasing

Caster sugar, for greasing

100g (3½oz) raspberry jam

2 punnets fresh raspberries

120g (4oz) caster sugar

70g (2½oz) cornflour

100ml water

Meringue topping

3 egg whites

120g (4oz) sugar

Pinch cream of tartar

Soufflé

4 egg whites

90g (3oz) sugar

Extra fresh raspberries, double cream or
ice cream to serve

Preheat oven to 180°C (350°F) and grease 6 soufflé ramekins with butter, taking care to grease to the very edge. Cover with caster sugar. Brush sides with raspberry jam and set aside on a baking tray.

Crush raspberries with caster sugar. Place into a small pan with water and bring to the boil. Mix cornflour with a little water to form a paste and add to the raspberries. Cook mixture until thick; cool completely and set aside.

To make the meringue topping, whisk the eggs to a firm peak and add the sugar and cream of tartar. Continue to whisk for 5 minutes until shiny. Spoon into a piping bag fitted with a small nozzle.

To make the soufflé, beat egg whites in an electric mixer until stiff peaks form. Add sugar and mix until shiny and very stiff. Fold into raspberry mixture and spoon evenly into ramekins. Cut the top square with the back of a knife.

Pipe plain meringue over the top of each soufflé. Bake for 8–12 minutes or until fully risen. Remove and dust with icing sugar.

Serve immediately with extra fresh raspberries and double cream, or ice cream.

HOT FRENCH CHOCOLATE SOUFFLÉ

SERVES 6

Preheat oven to 180°C (350°F) and grease 6 soufflé ramekins with butter; dust inside of ramekins with caster sugar then cocoa powder and shake out any excess. Set aside on a baking tray.

Bring milk and sugar to the boil in a medium saucepan and stir in sifted cocoa and flour until well combined. Reduce heat to medium and cook, stirring constantly, until mixture is smooth and shiny. Spoon chocolate mixture and chocolate pieces into a food processor and process until smooth and chocolate has melted. Transfer to a mixing bowl.

To make the soufflé, beat egg whites in an electric mixer until stiff peaks form. Add sugar and mix until shiny and very stiff. Fold into chocolate mixture and spoon evenly into ramekins. Cut the top square with the back of a knife.

Bake for 8–12 minutes, or until fully risen. Remove and dust with icing sugar and cocoa. Serve immediately with cream or chocolate ice cream.

Butter, caster sugar and cocoa powder for lining moulds

500ml (16fl oz) milk

50g (1½oz) sugar

50g (1½oz) cocoa powder

2 tablespoons plain flour

50g (1½oz) dark (at least 66% cocoa) chocolate buttons

Icing sugar and cocoa powder for dusting

Soufflé

4 egg whites

90g (3oz) sugar

Cream or chocolate ice cream, to serve

BANANA AND CITRUS SOUFFLÉ WITH RICH CHOCOLATE SAUCE

SERVES 6

Softened butter and caster sugar, for greasing

Rich chocolate sauce

300ml (10fl oz) cream

75g (2½oz) caster sugar

1 vanilla bean, split

150g (5oz) dark chocolate, chopped

Soufflé

2 large ripe bananas

2 tablespoons leatherwood honey

Zest of 1 orange and 1 lime

4 egg whites

100g (3½oz) sugar

Icing sugar, to serve

Preheat oven to 200°C (400°F) and grease 6 soufflé ramekins with butter, taking care to grease to the very edge. Line the insides of the ramekins with caster sugar and place onto a baking tray.

For the chocolate sauce, bring cream, sugar and vanilla bean to the boil, making sure that the sugar has dissolved. Pour hot cream over the chopped chocolate and mix until smooth and thick; set aside.

To make the soufflé, mash banana and mix with honey and citrus zest. Beat the egg white in an electric mixer until stiff peaks form. Add sugar and mix until shiny and very stiff. Fold into banana mixture and spoon evenly into ramekins. Cut the top square with the back of a knife.

Bake for 8–12 minutes, or until fully risen. Remove and dust with icing sugar. Serve immediately with the hot chocolate sauce.

PASSIONFRUIT SOUFFLÉ

SERVES 6

Passionfruit base

Butter and caster sugar, for greasing

250ml (9fl oz) passionfruit pulp

120g (4oz) sugar

70g (2½oz) cornflour

Soufflé

4 egg whites

90g (3oz) caster sugar

Icing sugar, to serve

Preheat oven to 180°C (350°F) and grease 6 soufflé ramekins with butter, taking care to grease to the very edge. Cover with caster sugar. Set aside on a baking tray.

Heat passionfruit pulp with sugar in a small saucepan until sugar has dissolved. Mix the cornflour with a little water to form a smooth paste and stir into saucepan; cook for 5 minutes or until thick. Set aside and leave to cool completely.

Beat egg whites in an electric mixer until stiff peaks form. Gradually add sugar and continue beating until shiny and stiff. Carefully fold egg whites into the passionfruit mix and spoon evenly into ramekins. Cut the top square with the back of a knife.

Bake for 8–12 minutes, or until fully risen. Remove and dust with icing sugar. Serve immediately.

ICED SUMMER FRUIT SALAD

SERVES 4-6

Fruit is never off the menu. Just change the fruit to suit the season.

To make the granita, bring 500ml (16fl oz) water to the boil, add sugar and simmer until sugar has dissolved. Allow to cool. Place mint and sugar syrup into a blender and pulse until smooth. Strain and freeze.

Combine passionfruit and syrup and bring to the boil. Stir in agar agar and mix to dissolve. Pour into a small shallow tray and refrigerate until just set. Using a whisk, stir unset jelly until broken up.

Carefully cut the fresh ripe fruit into very small dice and combine with the chopped jelly and crushed ice. Spoon into a serving glass. Pour in some cold sugar syrup and serve with a scoop of mint granita.

Mint granita

350g (11 ½oz) caster sugar

2 bunches mint, leaves picked

Passionfruit agar agar

4 fresh passionfruit, pulp removed

500ml (16fl oz) sugar syrup (see Basics)

15g (1 ½oz) agar agar or 2 leaves of gelatine

Fruit Salad

1 mango, peeled

8 strawberries, hulled and cut in half

1 kiwi fruit, peeled

1 small sugar banana, peeled

4 fresh lychees, peeled

Crushed ice, to serve

250ml (9fl oz) cold sugar syrup, to serve (see Basics)

ROASTED LATE SUMMER FRUIT SALAD

SERVES 4-6

Place 300ml (10fl oz) water, sugar and spices into a large deep pan and bring to the boil over medium/high heat. Simmer for 10 minutes or until sugar has dissolved and mixture is syrupy. Turn off heat and add fruit, ensuring that it is submerged. Stand for 10 minutes and strain, reserving syrup.

Return syrup to heat and simmer until reduced by one-third.

Preheat oven to 160°C (325°F) and lay fruit into a large deep baking dish. Roast fruit for 10–15 minutes, turning fruit halfway. Remove and cool in dish.

Meanwhile, beat ricotta with sugar, cream and vanilla until thick.

To serve, spoon fruit into serving glasses and layer with ricotta cream and some of the syrup.

300g (10½oz) sugar

1 lemon, sliced

1 cinnamon quill

2 star anise

4 ripe peaches, halved and stone removed

8 plums, halved and stone removed

6 black cherries (can be preserved)

6 figs, halved

4 nectarines, halved and stone removed

1 bunch rhubarb, trimmed and stalks cut in half

60g (2oz) roasted whole almonds

Ricotta cream

200g (7oz) fresh ricotta

75g (2½oz) caster sugar

100ml (3½fl oz) cream

1 vanilla bean, split lengthways and seeds scraped

Far left: Iced Summer Fruit Salad

Left: Roasted Late Summer Fruit Salad.

POACHED CHERRIES, CHOCOLATE AND CREAM

SERVES 6

This is a great alternative to Christmas pudding.

In a small saucepan, dissolve 180g (6½oz) of caster sugar with 200ml (7fl oz) water, add to that a slice of red chilli, a clove, a star anise and a vanilla bean. Cook for 5 minutes, then add the fresh cherries. Cook for 2 minutes, then remove from the heat and allow the cherries to cool in the syrup.

In a small bowl, mix together the cream and the mascarpone with the caster sugar. Whisk to a thick cream.

In a martini glass or serving bowl, place some crushed macaroon biscuits. Drizzle over some Baileys or your favourite liqueur. Then add a layer of the cream and then a layer of the poached cherries, adding more biscuits if you like. Once the bowls are almost full, place them into the fridge for an hour.

Make the chocolate sauce. In a mortar and pestle, grind together nutmeg, sugar, star anise and the clove.

In a small saucepan bring the cream to the boil. Add the spiced sugar and dissolve. Pour this over the chocolate and mix well until smooth. Allow to cool slightly.

To serve, pour the spiced chocolate sauce over the dessert, and place some fresh cherries on the top. Grate with chocolate and dust with icing sugar.

Poached cherries

180g (6½oz) caster sugar

1 red chilli, sliced

1 clove

1 star anise

1 vanilla bean

100g (3½oz) fresh cherries

Cream

400ml (14fl oz) cream

300g (10½ oz) mascarpone cream

100g (3½oz) caster sugar

6 x chocolate macaroons or biscuits

Baileys Irish Cream or Kahlua

Chocolate sauce

Grated nutmeg

100g (3½oz) caster sugar

1 star anise

1 clove

200ml (7fl oz) cream

100g (3½oz) dark chocolate

1 piece chocolate for grating

Icing sugar shaker

SPICED APPLES WITH SEMOLINA PUDDING, APPLE PIE SPICED SYRUP

SERVES 6

Spiced baked apples

50g (1½oz) butter

150g (5oz) brown sugar

Pinch cinnamon, ground

Pinch ginger, ground

Pinch cloves, ground

Pinch nutmeg, ground

6 apples, peeled, cored and quartered

Semolina pudding

700ml (23fl oz) milk

1 vanilla pod, split lengthways

2 tablespoons honey

75g (2½oz) caster sugar

60g (2oz) fine white semolina

Apple pie spiced syrup

150g (5oz) caster sugar

1 cinnamon stick

1 vanilla pod

Pinch ginger, ground

Pinch nutmeg, ground

1 clove

4 egg whites

75g (2½oz) caster sugar

Double cream, to serve

To make the spiced apples, place butter, sugar and spices in a large deep saucepan and stir over medium heat until both butter and sugar have melted and spices are fragrant. Add apples and toss to coat. Cook for 30 minutes, or until soft and toffee-like. Cool and set aside.

Preheat oven to 160°C (325°F) and grease a medium rectangular baking dish.

Heat milk, vanilla, honey and sugar over medium/high heat until milk comes to the boil. Gradually stir in semolina and cook until thickened (about 10 minutes). Remove and cool slightly.

To make the syrup, combine sugar and 150ml (5fl oz) water with spices and simmer for 5 minutes or until sugar has dissolved. Set aside.

In a clean bowl, beat egg whites and half the caster sugar with electric beaters to stiff peaks. Fold the semolina mixture through carefully and spoon into the prepared dish. Top with caramelised apples and bake for 30 minutes, until golden and cooked. The semolina will rise like a soufflé. Serve hot with the warm syrup and a large spoon of double cream.

PEACH BELLINI FRAPPÉ

SERVES 4

Half dessert half drink, this frappé is great in summer when peaches are at their best.

To make the peach sorbet, place peaches, sugar, 250ml (9fl oz) water and vanilla into a saucepan. Bring to the boil to dissolve sugar. Cool slightly and place in a food processor; pulse until puréed. Add lemon juice and peach liqueur. Pour into a deep dish, cover and freeze for 2 hours.

For the jelly, soak gelatine in cold water until soft. Puree raspberries until smooth and heat gently in a small saucepan with the sugar syrup. Squeeze out excess water from gelatine and stir into warm raspberry mixture. Add champagne and vanilla paste and mix well. Pour into a small bowl and refrigerate until set.

Preheat oven to 180°C (350°F). Cut peaches into slices, dust with icing sugar and cook in a hot oven until lightly caramelised. Remove and set aside.

To serve, arrange roasted peaches around the edges of small glass bowls. Spoon jelly in the base of each glass. Scoop a ball of frozen peach sorbet and place into the centre. Serve to the table and pour over champagne in front of your guests.

Peach sorbet

600g (1lb 3½oz) ripe white peaches, peeled, pitted and chopped

300g (10oz) caster sugar

1 lemon, juiced

1 tablespoon peach liqueur

Raspberry and champagne jelly

4 gelatine sheets

400g (13oz) fresh ripe raspberries

100ml (3½fl oz) cold sugar syrup (see Basics)

500ml (16fl oz) champagne

½ teaspoon vanilla paste

Roasted white peaches

4 ripe white peaches

Icing sugar

French champagne, to serve

POACHED VANILLA AND GINGER STRAWBERRIES WITH CRUNCH CRUMBLE BISCUITS AND CUSTARD

SERVES 4

These biscuits are great as petits four with coffee.

Crunch crumble biscuit

350g (11½oz) caster sugar

100g (3½oz) almonds, ground

150g (5oz) walnuts, finely chopped

Pinch cinnamon, ground

Pinch ginger, ground

Pinch nutmeg, ground

90g (3oz) softened butter

3 egg whites

60g (2¼oz) caster sugar

Icing sugar, for dusting

Custard

200ml (7fl oz) thickened cream

100ml (3½fl oz) milk

50g (1½oz) caster sugar

1 teaspoon vanilla extract

3 egg yolks

Poached vanilla ginger strawberries

400g (13oz) caster sugar

1 vanilla bean, split lengthways

2cm (¾in) piece fresh ginger, peeled and sliced

2 x 250g (8oz) punnets strawberries, hulled and washed

Preheat oven to 180°C (350°F) and line a baking tray with baking paper.

For the biscuits, place sugar into a small saucepan and cook over medium-low heat until a medium dark caramel forms. Remove from heat and cool slightly. Stir in nuts, spices and softened butter.

Whisk egg whites to soft peaks stage, add 60g (2¼oz) caster sugar and fold through biscuit mixture. Stir with a wooden spoon until well incorporated. Roll teaspoons of mixture into small balls and place onto prepared baking tray. Bake for 4 minutes, or until lightly coloured. While still warm, roll in icing sugar.

To make the custard, place the cream, milk, sugar and vanilla extract in a small saucepan and bring to the boil. Whisk the egg yolks together and stir in boiling cream mix. Return to pan and cook over low heat and until it starts to thicken. Remove and cool slightly.

Combine 500ml (16fl oz) water, sugar, vanilla bean and ginger in a saucepan and bring to the boil. Add strawberries and turn off heat; stand for 5 minutes. Scoop out strawberries with a slotted spoon and return syrup to stove. Simmer over high heat until reduced by half and syrupy.

To serve, spoon strawberries into serving glasses, add biscuits and spoon syrup over. Place warm custard into a foam canister loaded with gas, and spray thick aerated custard over the strawberries. Finish with the strawberry syrup.

BAKED CHOCOLATE MOUSSE

SERVES 6-8

This is the best chocolate cake I have ever tasted. It is a very difficult recipe to get right, but once you have made it a few times you will make it forever. And even the mistakes taste great!

Preheat oven to 180°C (350°F) and grease a 20cm (8in) ceramic baking dish.

Whisk eggs and 100g (3½oz) of the sugar together in the bowl of a mixmaster. Beat on medium speed for 10 minutes or until light, fluffy and doubled in size.

Place remaining sugar and 125ml (4½fl oz) water into a bowl over a saucepan of simmering water. Stir until sugar has dissolved. Add butter and chocolate and stir occasionally until melted and smooth. Remove from heat and cool completely.

Carefully fold chocolate mixture into beaten egg until just mixed through. Pour into prepared dish. Place into a larger baking dish filled with enough boiling water to come to the top of the ceramic dish. Bake for 1¼ hours, or until just set. Remove from pan and cool completely in dish for 1 hour.

Turn out and cut into portions. Serve with whipped cream and strawberry salad.

5 whole eggs

280g (10oz) caster sugar

225g (7oz) unsalted butter, diced

340g (11½oz) dark couverture (71%) chocolate, chopped

Whipped cream and strawberries, to serve

ICED PINEAPPLE SEMI-FREDDO AND GLASS BISCUIT SANDWICH

SERVES 6

Pineapple parfait

1 pineapple, peeled (approx 300g (10oz) flesh)

250g (8oz) caster sugar

30g (1oz) cornflour

4 egg whites

75g (2½oz) caster sugar

400ml (13fl oz) thickened cream, whipped

Glass Biscuits

250g (8oz) butter

225g (7oz) glucose syrup

225g (7oz) plain flour

Fresh peeled lychees and pomegranate seeds, to serve

Preheat oven to 180°C (350°F).

Cut the pineapple into thick slices and place into a deep dish. Bring 300ml (10fl oz) water and sugar to the boil over high heat. Pour over pineapple to cover; bake for 1 hour or until pineapple is soft. Cool and drain, reserving remaining syrup, and process in a food processor until smooth.

Place purée into a saucepan and bring to the boil over medium heat. Dissolve cornflour into a little water and stir into the pineapple; cook until it thickens. Remove and cool completely.

Line a baking tray with baking paper. Beat egg whites until stiff peaks form, add caster sugar and beat until well combined. Fold through cooled pineapple mixture and whipped cream, taking care not to overmix. Place spoonfuls of mixture into small, 12cm (5in) wide dishes or pastry rings and freeze for 2 hours until hard.

Melt butter and glucose together and pour into a mixing bowl. Stir in flour to form a dough. Tip onto a lightly floured surface and roll out into small balls. Place onto greased and lined baking trays and bake for 6 minutes, until spread and thin. Remove from the oven, and while still hot cut, with a 12cm (5in) cutter. Allow to cool.

To serve, unmould pineapple parfaits and sandwich between biscuits. Serve with lychees and pomegranate seeds.

CHEESE

Never serve a cheese platter to start a meal. It is high in fat and can have dominating lingering flavours. It should be served at the correct temperature at the end of a meal.

A cheese course says a lot about you as an entertainer. One great piece of cheese is better than a selection of ordinary ones. Be generous and always buy a bigger piece than you think you may need. Build up a collection of pickles and preserved fruits to add your own touch.

Some simple cheese tips

- Serving cheese is all about the temperature. Bring cheese to room temperature slowly over a couple of hours and allow soft cheeses to melt a little.
- When you buy cheese, ask about its age and ripeness. Try not to buy too far in advance.
- People who sell cheese love to talk about it, so get to know them and taste as you go.
- I like to balance the saltiness of cheese with the tartness or sweetness of fruit.
- Keep your breads or crackers high quality but plain in flavour.
- Store your cheese by wrapping individually in greaseproof paper in a sealed container in the fridge.

PARMESAN AND BLACK PEPPER BISCUITS

MAKES 36 SMALL BISCUITS

Combine flour, baking powder, salt, cayenne and 1 teaspoon of pepper into a food processor and pulse until thoroughly mixed.

Add softened butter and parmesan and process until it forms a ball. With floured hands, remove dough and roll into a cylinder approximately 15cm (6in) long and 6cm (2½in) wide. Wrap in plastic wrap and refrigerate for 2 hours or freeze until required.

Preheat oven to 180°C (350°F) and line two baking trays with baking paper.

Cut dough into 3mm thick slices and place onto baking trays. Sprinkle each biscuit with a little of the remaining pepper and sea salt and bake for 15 minutes or until golden. Allow biscuits to stand for 5 minutes on the tray before cooling completely on wire racks.

Place in airtight containers and consume within 24 hours.

300g (10½oz) plain flour

1 teaspoon baking powder

1 pinch of sea salt, plus extra for garnish

1 pinch cayenne pepper

2 teaspoons freshly ground black pepper

180g (3oz) softened butter

80g (3oz) freshly grated parmesan

JINDI TRIPLE CREAM WITH SOFT POACHED QUINCE PASTE

Jindi triple cream has a round shape with a smooth velvety, white penicillin rind. It has a rich and buttery texture with a sweet taste. The flavour has a hint of mushrooms. The maturing period is 4 to 5 weeks.

Country / region = Australia / Gippsland Victoria
Milk = Cow
Texture = Soft

Soft poached quince paste

Serves 1 small jar

250g (8oz) caster sugar

1 star anise

1 stick cinnamon

3 medium-sized ripe quinces

1 lemon

Bring 300ml (10fl oz) water, sugar and spices to the boil.

Peel and core the quinces, retaining the skin and core. Place these into a small piece of muslin cloth; tie up to enclose. Drop muslin bag into the cooking liquid.

Cut the quince into 2cm (¾in) dice and place in the liquid. Simmer on the stove or bake in a medium oven in a casserole dish for 1 hour, or until tender. Remove the muslin bag and whole spices and discard.

Drain the liquid and return the quince to the heat. Mash the hot quince with the back of a fork until broken down. Return the poaching liquid to the pan and simmer for 30 minutes, stirring well, until a smooth paste is formed. Remove and place in a container until required.

TALLEGIO WITH WALNUT PRALINE

Tallegio is a buttery, delicate, semi-soft cow's milk cheese from Italy. It usually has a square shape. The cheese has a special taste and aroma; the crust is pinkish-grey and the paste is white, supple and fruity. It ripens in 25-50 days and has a fat content of 48%.

Tallegio is known as Stracchino from the Italian stracche (fatigued), which refers to the cows after travelling back to the valley from their grazing season in the high pasture.

Country / region = Italy / Lombardy
Milk = Cow
Fat content = 48%

Warm sugar in a heavy-based saucepan over a low heat until melted and forming a dark caramel.

Toast the walnuts in a medium oven (180°C (350°F)) and add to the caramel; mix through. Mixture will be hard at this stage. Quickly add the vinegar and continue to mix until all the walnuts are coated and vinegar has evaporated.

Turn walnuts onto an oiled tray, separating nuts from each other. Cool completely.

Store in a dry, airtight container for 2-3 days.

Walnut praline

Serves 150g (5oz)

250g (8oz) caster sugar

150g (5oz) good-quality walnut halves, unbroken

60ml (2fl oz) cabernet vinegar

QUICKE'S SHAVED CHEDDAR WITH CRISP PINK APPLE AND CELERY SALAD

Made from cow's milk, Quicke's cheddar is a relatively hard, pale yellow to off white, sharp-tasting cheese, originating in the English village of Cheddar in Somerset.
Its texture is hard to semi hard, and it is aged for a minimum of twelve months.

Country = England
Milk = Cow
Texture = Hard / Semi Hard

Crisp pink apple and celery salad

Serves 4

90ml (3fl oz) sour cream

2 tablespoons olive oil

Pinch English mustard

Sea salt and pepper

1 stick celery heart

2 pink lady apples

Whisk the cream, olive oil and mustard together and season.

Cut the celery into thin slivers and cover with a damp paper towel.

Remove the cores from the apples and slice thinly into a small bowl. Add the celery and coat lightly with the dressing. Shave the cheddar using a cheese slice and serve with the salad.

COLSTON BASSETT STILTON WITH TEA-SOAKED PRUNES

This cheese, from Nottingham, England, is the finest and creamiest example of Stilton available today. Made with the milk from five herds of cows grazing near Colston Bassett dairy, this handmade Stilton develops a fine, bark-like natural rind and ample blue veining. It is aged for four months. Stilton is a blue mould cheese with a rich and mellow flavour and a piquant aftertaste.

Country = England
Milk = Cow
Texture = Semi Hard

Bring 200ml (7fl oz) water and sugar to the boil. Add the cinnamon quill and a strip of the lemon skin; simmer for 5 minutes. Remove from heat and add the tea bag; steep for 20 minutes.

Reheat liquid and pour over the prunes. Allow to soak for a minimum of 2 hours, or overnight.

Drain and serve warm with the cheese.

Tea-soaked prunes

Serves 4

100g (3½oz) caster sugar
1 cinnamon quill
1 lemon
1 teabag of black tea
150g (5oz) dried prunes

PETITS FOURS

Small little sweet treats are often forgotten when entertaining; you should at least have a bar of good chocolate available or some toffee to smash up and serve on a small plate.

If you take the time to bake something, however, it will be greatly appreciated.

Presentation is everything at the end of the meal, so lay these treats onto nice plates, or even pile them into a bowl or a small box.

MEXICAN WEDDING BISCUITS

MAKES: 36 BISCUITS

Preheat oven to 180°C (350°F) and line 2 baking trays with baking paper.

Beat butter and sugar together until pale and creamy. Add brandy and mix well.

Combine almonds, walnuts and flour together and fold into butter mixture to form a sticky dough. Roll dough into walnut-sized balls and place onto prepared trays, leaving a few centimetres between each one so that the biscuits can spread a little as they cook.

Bake for 15–20 minutes, swapping trays halfway through the cooking time. Biscuits should be firm and golden. Remove from oven and, while hot, drop the biscuits into a deep tray of icing sugar. They will absorb some of the icing sugar and form a lovely creamy covering.

125g (4½oz) unsalted butter, softened

90g (3oz) caster sugar

2 tablespoons brandy

60g (2oz) almonds, ground

60g (2oz) walnuts, finely chopped

150g (5oz) plain flour, sifted

300g (10oz) icing sugar, for coating

VANILLA BRÛLÉE

FILLS 18 TARTLETS

300ml (10fl oz) cream

1 vanilla pod

165g (5½oz) caster sugar

4 egg yolks

1 quantity of sweet pastry cases (see page 230)

Preheat oven to 160°C (325°F).

Bring cream, vanilla and 75g (2½oz) of the caster sugar to the boil in a small saucepan over medium heat, ensuring sugar is dissolved.

Whisk eggs yolks until thick and pale in a mixing bowl; pour over the hot cream and mix well. Pour into a small baking dish and place into water bath; bake for 20 minutes. Remove from oven and allow to cool in the fridge.

Spoon the crème brûlée custard into the tartlets and smooth the top. Dust with remaining caster sugar and caramelise, using a blowtorch to create a crisp, dark caramel toffee crust.

HAZELNUT PRALINES IN DARK CHOCOLATE

MAKES: 36 PRALINES

Place sugar and 75ml (2½fl oz) water into a heavy-based saucepan and stir over medium heat until sugar dissolves. Once sugar has dissolved, increase heat to high and bring to the boil. Cook for 12–15 minutes, or until mixture is a light caramel colour.

Remove saucepan from heat and dip base immediately into cold water. Quickly add hazelnuts and stir gently. Pour onto a greased and lined baking tray. Allow to cool completely.

Using a rolling pin, break praline into bite-sized shards and store in an airtight container until required.

Melt chocolate in a bowl over a saucepan of simmering water until just melted. Remove and cool slightly. Dip praline shards into melted chocolate, then into cocoa powder. Cool on a wire rack.

250g (8oz) caster sugar

150g (5oz) roasted hazelnuts

100g (3½oz) good-quality dark chocolate

75g (2½oz) dark cocoa powder

SWEET PASTRY CASES

MAKES: 36 SMALL TART CASES

225g (7oz) plain flour, plus extra for kneading

40g (1½oz) icing sugar

125g (4½oz) softened butter, plus extra for greasing

2 egg yolks

Combine flour, icing sugar and butter in a food processer and process until crumbly. Add egg yolks and 2 teaspoons of ice water and pulse until dough just comes together. Tip onto a lightly floured work surface and bring dough together to form a soft ball. Wrap in plastic wrap and refrigerate for 30 minutes.

Preheat oven to 200°C (400°F) and grease 18 small 5-8cm (2-3in) tart tins with butter.

Roll out pastry to 1cm (½in) thick and cut out with cookie cutters to fit tin size. Line tin with pastry and blind bake for 8 minutes. Remove and cool.

CHOCOLATE ORANGE TARTS

FILLS 18 TARTLETS

3 eggs

Zest of 2 oranges

160ml (5½fl oz) thickened cream

165g (5½oz) caster sugar

60g (2oz) dark chocolate, melted

2 tablespoons cocoa powder

2 tablespoons Grand Marnier

1 quantity of sweet pastry cases (see page 230)

Preheat oven to 180°C (350°F).

Whisk eggs, zest, cream and sugar together until thoroughly mixed. Stir in melted chocolate, cocoa powder and Grand Marnier. Skim off any air bubbles.

Spoon into tartlet cases and bake for 15 minutes, or until mixture ripples when tarts are shaken.

Turn oven off and leave for 5 minutes. Remove and cool completely.

PISTACHIO MACARON GLACÉ

MAKES 60 SMALL OR 30 LARGE MACARONS

Preheat oven to 150°C (300°F). Blend almond meal and icing sugar and process as fine as possible. Sift twice through a fine sieve.

In a separate bowl, beat eggs whites, crème of tartar and caster sugar to make firm peaks. Whisk in food colouring and pistachio paste. Fold in the dry mixture. Do not over mix.

Place into piping bag and pipe onto silicon paper on baking tray. Bang the base of the trays on your hand to evenly spread out the mixture. Allow to dry for 2-3 hours, then bake for 10 minutes. Remove from oven and allow to cool.

For the pistachio filling, bring the cream to the boil and pour over white chocolate. Stir until all chocolate is melted. Whisk in the pistachio paste and cool, put in piping bag.

Pipe a small amount of filling onto one biscuit and stick two of them together.

200g (7oz) almond meal

240g (8½oz) icing sugar

140g egg whites (approx 5 eggs)

100g (3½oz) caster sugar

Pinch cream of tartar

1 drop green food colouring

1 tablespoon pistachio paste

Pistachio filling

200g (7oz) pure cream

400g (14oz) white chocolate

40g (1½oz) pistachio paste

LEMON MERINGUE TARTLETS

FILLS 18 TARTLETS

Lemon curd

150ml (5fl oz) lemon juice

4 egg yolks

100g (3½oz) caster sugar

100g (3½oz) butter, diced

Meringue

3 egg whites

75g (2½oz) caster sugar

1 quantity of sweet pastry cases (see page 230)

Icing sugar, for dusting

Place lemon juice, eggs and sugar into a mixing bowl and cook, stirring constantly, over a saucepan of simmering water until thick. Stir in butter and leave to cool, then refrigerate and set. Spoon lemon curd evenly into prepared pastry tartlets.

To make the meringue, beat egg whites with an electric beater until soft peaks form. Gradually add sugar, a little at a time, until well incorporated and meringue is stiff and glossy.

Spoon into a piping bag and pipe on top of the tartlets.

Using a blow torch or a very hot grill, brown meringue for 30 seconds until golden and dust with icing sugar.

CRISP BUTTER CAKES

MAKES: 36 SMALL CAKES

Preheat oven to 200°C (400°F).

Soak raisins in brandy for 1 hour or until plump; drain and set aside.

Melt butter in a hot frying pan until just turning golden brown. Remove from heat and allow to cool.

Combine icing sugar, almonds and flour in a large mixing bowl. Make a well in the centre and add egg whites; mix well to combine.

Stir in melted butter and beat until completely incorporated. Pipe the mixture into small 5cm (2in) greased baking tins and place a drained raisin on the top of each one.

Bake for 5 minutes, or until crisp and brown. The top of the biscuits should rise slightly. Wait to cool. Remove from the moulds using a small knife. Dust heavily with icing sugar and serve hot with coffee.

20g (²/₃oz) raisins

100ml (3½fl oz) brandy

200g (7oz) unsalted butter, plus extra for greasing

200g (7oz) icing sugar

100g (3½oz) almonds, ground

80g (3oz) plain flour

5 egg whites, lightly beaten

Icing sugar, for dusting

COCKTAILS

A glass of quality fizz on arrival is always a winner, but a simple, elegant cocktail really gets any event going.

Everyone has their favourite and these are mine. Their beauty is in their freshness and clarity; you must use the very best or your personal favourite spirits. Take the time to press all juices fresh, and pick herbs at the last minute. Use fresh, distilled water to make ice if you can.

MOJITO

1 LARGE DRINK

1 fresh lime, cut in wedges

2 tablespoons simple syrup (see Basics)

½ bunch fresh mint

60ml (2fl oz) Bacardi 8

Dash soda water

Ice from distilled water

1 stick sugar cane

In a glass, muddle the limes with the sugar syrup and mint leaves. Pour over the Bacardi and the soda water. Add the ice and stir well together. Garnish with a piece of fresh sugar cane.

MARGARITA

1 LARGE DRINK

Place a generous amount of ice in a cocktail shaker. Pour in all ingredients and shake well. Strain into a salt-rimmed glass.

Ice from distilled water

50ml (1¾fl oz) Patron silver Tequila

1½ tablespoons Patron citronge

1½ tablespoons freshly squeezed lemon juice

1½ tablespoons freshly squeezed lime juice

1½ tablespoons freshly squeezed orange juice

2 tablespoons simple syrup (see Basics)

1 teaspoon Murray River salt, finely ground

GINNY, GIN GIN AND TONIC

1 LARGE DRINK

Ice from distilled water

Zest of Ruby grapefruit

50ml (1¾fl oz) Tanqueray 10 Gin

Juniper berries

Baby coriander leaves

1 fresh bay leaf

Slice of fresh lime

Freshly milled black pepper

Nasturtium leaves or edible flowers

250ml (9fl oz) tonic to taste

Place a large piece of ice into a large round glass. Squeeze and release the zest of the grapefruit skin. Pour in the gin and place the remaining garnishes on the ice. Serve the chilled tonic water on the side.

WATERMELON MARTINI

1 LARGE MARTINI

Place all ingredients, except for anise Ricard, into a cocktail shaker with half a glass of ice and shake well.

Pour Ricard into martini glass and shake out to line glass.

Pour martini into glass and serve with a ball of chilled watermelon.

60ml (2fl oz) watermelon juice

50ml (1¾fl oz) Grey Goose la poire vodka

2 tablespoons simple syrup (see Basics)

Ice made from distilled water

5ml (1 teaspoon) anise Ricard

Chilled watermelon, to serve

CLASSIC MARTINI

1 LARGE MARTINI

5ml (1 teaspoon) vermouth

60ml (2fl oz) vodka, frozen

½ lime, cut into zest strips

Pour vermouth into glass and swirl around to line glass. Pour out residue. Pour in frozen vodka.

Squeeze the zest of 2 lime wedges three times around the rim and serve.

(This is the classic martini recipe from the St James Hotel in London.)

FROZEN VODKA ROCKS

1 LARGE DRINK

Place the ice into a short glass. Squeeze the fresh lime into the glass, making sure you release the zest oil from the skin.

Pour over frozen vodka and top with tonic water.

Ice cubes made from distilled water

½ fresh lime, cut in wedges

50ml (1¾fl oz) Grey Goose vodka, frozen

250ml (9fl oz) tonic, to taste

BASICS

Use this as a starter for your own basic recipe collection.

OLIVE OIL MAYONNAISE

MAKES: 10 PORTIONS

3 egg yolks

1 teaspoon Dijon mustard

2 teaspoons lemon juice

100ml (3½fl oz) extra virgin olive oil

150ml (5fl oz) sunflower oil

Sea salt and freshly ground white
pepper

Whisk egg yolks, mustard and lemon juice together in a small bowl until well combined. Slowly drizzle in oils, a little at a time, while whisking continuously.

Mayonnaise should thicken and become glossy. If mayonnaise is too thick, loosen with a little warm water or extra lemon juice.

Season with salt and pepper, cover and refrigerate for up to a week.

NOTE: bring all ingredients to room temperature to lower the risk of the mayonnaise splitting.

WALNUT PESTO

MAKES: 10 PORTIONS

Place walnuts, garlic and parsley into a mortar and pound with a pestle until smooth. Gradually add oil and mix well. Season with salt and pepper and set aside.

Alternatively, place walnuts, garlic and parsley into the bowl of a food processor and process until broken down. While motor is still running, drizzle in oil to form a thick sauce. Season with salt and pepper.

Keep in fridge for 3 days.

100g (3½oz) walnuts, toasted

1 clove garlic, chopped

3 bunches flat parsley

90ml (3fl oz) olive oil

Sea salt and pepper

ROASTED TOMATO JAM

MAKES: 10 PORTIONS

6 ripe tomatoes, cut in half

Sea salt and freshly ground black
pepper

80ml (3oz) olive oil

1 onion, finely diced

1 clove garlic, crushed

3 tablespoons palm sugar

½ teaspoon cumin, ground

1 pinch fennel seeds, ground

Preheat oven to 180°C (350°F).

Place tomatoes, cut side up, onto a lined baking tray. Season with salt and pepper and roast in oven for 30 minutes. Remove and chop coarsely.

Heat oil in a frying pan and add onion and garlic; cook for 3 minutes to soften and stir in palm sugar and roasted chopped tomatoes. Add spices and stir well to combine. Cook for a further 10 minutes.

Remove and purée until smooth. Return to the same pan and continue cooking until the tomato jam is the consistency of a thick paste. Adjust seasoning, remove and cool completely.

ROASTED BLACK PEPPER OIL

MAKES 100ML (3½FL OZ)

Dry roast the peppercorns in a frying pan for 5 minutes or until fragrant. Cover with the olive oil and remove from heat. Tip into a mortar and cool for 1–2 minutes. Grind with a pestle to crush the peppercorns. Set aside to cool completely.

1 tablespoon black peppercorns

100ml (3½fl oz) olive oil

SUGAR SYRUP

500g (1lb) sugar

500ml (16fl oz) water

1 vanilla bean

½ orange, sliced

Bring to the boil over medium heat until sugar has dissolved and syrup is clear. Add the vanilla bean and the orange slices and simmer for 10 minutes. Strain and cool completely.

Will keep for 14 days.

SIMPLE SYRUP

This is used for cocktails.

500g (1lb) sugar

500ml (16fl oz) water

Bring to the boil over medium heat until sugar has dissolved and syrup is clear. Strain and cool completely.

Will keep for 14 days.

PASTA DOUGH

MAKES: 10 PORTIONS

Place flour and salt into a mound on a clean work surface and make a well in the centre. Crack eggs into the centre and add oil. With a fork, gently work eggs into flour, gradually drawing the flour in as you go, until the dough is thick.

Bring dough together and knead for 5 minutes or until smooth and elastic. Shape the dough into a disc, lightly coat in flour and wrap in plastic wrap. Set aside for ½ hour to rest.

Divide dough into 4 equal portions. Set the pasta machine on the widest setting and coat the rollers lightly in flour. Feed one portion of dough through the machine. Repeat 6 times, folding pasta into thirds and turning 90 degrees to the pasta machine each time.

When dough is the same width as the machine, continue to feed the dough through, gradually narrowing the pasta machine to the smallest setting, 1 notch at a time, until dough is the correct thickness. The lowest setting is used for great eating pasta or ravioli. Dust pasta sheets with semolina and repeat with remaining dough.

Cut and shape pasta as required. Take care to keep dry.

400g (13oz) '00' flour, plus extra for kneading

Pinch salt

4 large eggs

3 tablespoons olive oil

Semolina, for dusting

GLOSSARY

AL DENTE - Literally means 'to the tooth', referring to correctly cooking pasta so that it is tender, but still firm to the bite.

BLANCH - To cook raw in boiling water for a very short time. The ingredients are then refreshed in cold water and drained.

BLIND BAKE - To bake a pie crust without a filling. There are several techniques used to ensure that the pie crust holds it shape when baked empty. Pie weights can be placed in the shell to keep it from puffing. The shell can be lined with foil and dried beans or peas. Pricking the crust with a fork before baking also helps the crust keep its shape.

CONFIT - This is a French word that is best translated as preserving. It historically refers to a meat submerged in fat and cooked slowly until very tender. Confit has recently been expanded to include slow cooking of meat, fish, fruit or vegetables in a flavoured oil such as olive oil.

DEVEIN - To remove the dark intestinal vein along the back of crustaceans, such as prawns.

DRY FRYING - Heating food in a pan without using any fat or oil. It can be used for foods such as nuts and, particularly, spices, as it helps to release the flavours.

FIRE (SCORCHED) - To release and burn the zest of citrus fruit, used in dressings and some desserts.

HARISSA PASTE - A fiery condiment made from grinding dried red chillies and garlic to a paste. Some versions of harissa include roasted red capsicums in the paste. Popular in Morocco, Tunisia and Algeria, harissa is often seasoned with ground cumin, ground caraway and ground coriander. Lemon juice and olive oil are used to moisten and thin the paste.

ISRAELI COUS COUS - Wheat-based baked pasta, originally produced in the shape of elongated rice grains and today mostly in the shape of round pearls. It is known as Israeli cous cous or Jerusalem cous cous and is one of the foods considered to be a unique Israeli culinary contribution.

KNEAD - A process to make bread dough mix become elastic and tender. It develops the gluten in the bread that traps the carbon dioxide produced by the yeast and makes bread rise. Pull the dough furthest away from you over and towards you, in a folding motion. Using your fist or the heels of your hands, push on the dough away from you so that it compresses and then stretches. Turn the dough about 45 degrees round and repeat. Continue till the dough is smooth and elastic and springs back when the surface is lightly pressed with a finger. Kneading can take a while, typically 10 minutes.

KNOCKING BACK - dough - The process of knocking back is usually to stick your fist into the risen dough, so that it collapses. Then knead for about a minute until all the cold surfaces have gone and the dough feels a uniform temperature.

MUDDLE - Cocktail ingredients are normally muddled, which means to combine them usually in the bottom of a mixing glass, by pressing them with a muddler before adding the liquids. A muddler is a long pestle, often shaped like a baseball bat.

MUSTARD FRUITS - A pungent condiment made with seasonal fruit, vinegar or citrus juices, mustard and spices. The perfect accompaniment for glazed baked hams and roasts.

PEDRO XIMÉNEZ SHERRY - Pedro Ximénez Sherry is a grape variety from Jerez in Spain. Traditionally, it is dried in the hot Spanish sun and used to make sherry and other fortified wines. This sherry is usually rich, sweet and dark in nature, with a strong taste of raisins and molasses.

PRESERVED LEMON - A condiment that is common in North African cuisine, especially Moroccan cuisine. Diced, quartered, halved, or whole lemons are pickled in a brine of water, lemon juice, and salt; occasionally spices are included as well. The pickle is allowed to ferment at room temperature for weeks or months before it is used. The pulp of the preserved lemon can be used in stews and sauces, but it is the peel (zest and pith together) that is most valued. The flavour is mildly tart but intensely lemony.

PROVE - To allow dough to rise after leavening agent has been added, usually covered with a cloth and left in a warm place.

SPONGING YEAST - Sponge is a wet batter that has yeast added to it. A starter is often called a sponge because the yeast has bubbles in it and makes the batter appear sponge-like.

SOFT PEAKS - When beating egg whites, a soft peak is reached when the beaters are pulled out of the whites and the peaks that form droop.

STIFF PEAKS - Always start with eggs at room temperature. Beat egg whites in a clean, grease-free bowl. When the beaters are lifted from the egg whites, peaks are formed that hold their shape. When egg whites have reached the stiff peak stage, they are opaque, thick and shiny, or glossy.

ZA'ATAR - A Middle Eastern spice mix of thyme, sumac, toasted sesame seed, and sometimes wild oregano. It is Arabic for the word 'thyme', after the seasoning's predominant ingredient. Olive oil is often added to make a spreadable paste, which is then served with everything from flatbreads to eggs to vegetables.

ACKNOWLEDGEMENTS

Sitting down to write a page of thanks and recognition to all the people who have helped me in life is a humbling experience and a great time to reflect.

I always thought it was just my own drive and determination that made things happen but in reality there are a lot of people who have helped and supported me throughout my life and career.

There are so many people to mention—chefs, friends, business associates, suppliers:

John and Peter Andrews, John Susman, Thomas Bucich, Simon Johnson, Tonci Farac, Sir Terence Conran, Joel Kissen, Des Gunewardener, David Bafsky, Michael Issenberg, Robert Murray, Iain Gray, Dave Wallace, Anthony Comino, David Hopcroft, Justin McLaren, Richard Latham, Liegh Moulds, Graeme Jones, Norbert Chabot, Cheong Tse, Martin Webb, Chris Galvin, Dave Sampson, Jess Ong, Andy Turner, Simon Sandall, Paul Wilson, Mark Stone, Dave Greenhill, Bill Magno, Ron Coleman, Geoff Janz; Alfonso and Alvaro Maccioni, Tal Eloss and James Denny, Steve Szabo.

To my 'teachers'

Grandmothers Ruby and Norah who taught me the seasons, the ripeness and the reward that cooking can give. Alan Humphries and Cliff Burgess, my lecturers, for pushing me harder than the other students. Head chefs, Serge Dansereau, Yves Farouz, David Miller, Bernard Cutts and Andre Schon.

To my friends

Ronny Truss a true friend and one of the most successful people I know on every level. Gordon Ramsay, my long-time friend who's still the same to me, but an inspiration. Sean Connolly, the most grounded star on the food planet. Michael Tafe, godfather to Charlie and one of the most talented chefs in Australia. Kerri-Anne Kennerly for inviting me on your show eight years ago to master the art of cooking on live TV in 2 minutes. Jamie Malcolm, a wonderfully talented man and genuine person. Caroline Dempsey, Matthew Melhuish and Tim Clarke for your friendship and professional wisdom.

Special mention to Matt Moran, my best mate. A real chef in every sense of the word. A caring, supportive and generous person.

To my business team

Jean-Christophe Bafoil for keeping Food Matrix a continued success. The entire Summit team for your loyalty and hard work and for putting up with me. Brett Luckens, my head chef, for keeping the ship on course: you're a great chef. Restaurant manager, Tim Claydon, and his team Frank , Maricia and Makram for your continuing committment and loyalty.

Sam Mandoukis at the NAB for recognising the opportunity and supporting the dream.

Mel Rais for keeping the books in order and the years of support through the thick and thin. Paul McGreal, my accountant, for always finding solutions and looking out for my best interests.

To the people who helped bring this book together. Thank you to New Holland Publishers, especially Fiona Schultz and Lliane Clarke. Michelle Lucia for helping with the recipes. Thanks to Emma Gough for her design, stylist Trish Hegarty, and photographers Graeme Gillies and Karen Watson for bringing it to life. Wonderful 'models': Matt, Alex, Tracey, Rowland, Ariana, Steve, Jamie and Selina.

Special mention to Steven McArthur (minister without portfolio!). My right-hand man. The most loyal, hard-working and committed person anyone could wish for in their business. Truly this book would never have happened without you.

To my very special family

My daughter Eloise (Squeeze) who is so precious to me and already has an amazing gift for cooking.

My son Charlie, who I believe will become the man I dream of being.

Dad, for instilling in me incredible self belief and an amazing work ethic.

My little sister Lisa, for looking after Mum while I chased my dreams.

Kay (my textbook perfect mother-in-law) for your love and support and remaining a positive force in our life—every step of the way.

Sam and Jan for your endless support. Thanks for loving our children and allowing Angela and I time to catch our breath now and then.

Tom, for allowing me to marry your daughter and being proud of our achievements.

A special mention to my mum, Lesley, who is nothing but proud of me. Working so hard for so long to make opportunities become reality. Thanks for teaching me to get up and try my best everyday.

Finally, to my wife Angela. My soul mate, best friend, the love of my life and still the most beautiful woman I have ever seen. You have been the greatest support and an amazing mother to our children. Thanks for holding my hand and embracing the risks. Together we can do anything.

INDEX

Aioli, roasted garlic   119
Angel hair shellfish pasta   127
Apple and celery salad   220
Apple pie spiced syrup   196
Apple salad   30
Asparagus salad pissladiere with grape fondue   101
Brunch   22
Baked chocolate mouse   205
Baked eggs with roast capsicum relish, beans
   and chorizo   39
Basics   252
Beef
   cheeks with stock pot carrots   149
   rare roast beef sandwich with gogonzola and
   pear salad   47
   summer carpaccio   90
   winter carpaccio   91
Bircher muesli with apple salad   30
Biscuits
   Mexican wedding   225
   parmesan and black pepper   215
Braised beef cheeks with stock pot carrots   149
Broccoli with fresh red chilli   170
Brulée, vanilla   226
Buffalo mozzarella with tomato and black olive
   tapenade   74
Canapés   52
Caesar salad   90
Capsicum relish   39
Champagne summer berry breakfast jelly   29
Cheese   210
Chicken
   cold set with artichoke and chickpea salad   33
   simple lemon with mint yoghurt   141
   slow cooked with orzo pasta and white beans   42
Chips with rosemary salt   166
Chocolate orange tarts   230
Cocktails   236
Cold set chicken, artichoke and chickpea salad   33
Cold-smoked hirimasa kingfish with miso dressing   75
Cress and herb salad with botrytis dressing   179
Crips-fried prawns with somin noodles   64
Crisp butter cakes   235
Desserts   180
Entrées   82

Eggs
   baked with roast capsicum relish, beans and
   chorizo   39
   scrambled with smoked trout   32
Fruit salad   191, 193
Garlic and parmesan bread   41
Glazed carrot with cumin   173
Goat's cheese and blood orange dip with sweet
   potato chips   106
Granita   57
Green beans with garlic, lemon thyme and shallots   174
Griled sirloin on the bone with salt brine and roasted
   mushroom   152
Grilled figs and stone fruit with ricotta and toast   36
Grilled veal chops with risotto   159
Hazlenut pralines in dark chocolate   227
Iced pineapple semi-freddo and glass biscuit   206
Iced summer fruit salad   191
Jam, roasted tomato   258
Kingfish
   cold-smoked hirimasa with spiced miso dressing   75
   with ocean trout and citrus dressing   69
Lamb
   slow cooked with poached cherries and cherry
   toffee   144
   slow-cooked warm salad   147
Lemon meringue tartlets   232
Lemon-spiced spatchcock with Israeli cous cous   138
Mains   116
Mashed potato with double cream and butter   169
Mayonnaise, olive oil   254
Mozzarella, beetroot and horseradish   115
My one-pot, one-bowl crab Napolitano pasta   46
Naked shellfish ravioli with squid bolognese   123
Oil, roasted black pepper   259
Olive oil bread   96
Olives, warm roasted with fennel, herbs and
   hand rolled bread stick   79
Onions, scorched   91
Oyster shots, with watermelon and ginger   59
Oysters
   with cabernet mignonette granita   58
   with cucumber tea granita   54
   with picked tomato granita   57
   fried   114
Parmesan and black pepper biscuits   215
Pasta dough   261
Pasta
   angel hair shellfish   127

one-pot, one-bowl crab Napolitano pasta 46

orzo pasta with slow cooked chicken and white beans 42

Peach bellini frappé 201

Peppered veal ribs with celeriac purée 154

Pesto, walnut 255

Petits Fours 222

Petuna cold-smoked ocean trout served with warm fennel broth 102

Pistachio macaron glacé 231

Poached cherries, chocolate and cream 195

Poached vanilla and ginger strawberries with crunch crumble biscuits and custard

Pork belly
crispy with baked stuffed apples 137
twice cooked with roasted apple marmalade 134

Potato pancakes with mandarin vodka-cured salmon, crème fraiche 62

Prawn minestrone with walnut pesto 86

Prawns
crisp-fried 64
spice roasted pumpkin with ricotta and 131

Quince paste, soft poached 218

Rare roast beef sandwich with gogonzola and pear salad 47

Rare veal and fennel involtini 72

Raspbery and ricotta soufflé pancake 26

Ricotta
souffle pancake and raspberry 26
with grilled figs and stone fruit on toast 36

Roasted apple marmalade 134

Roasted late summer fruit salad 193

Roasted mushroom and onion soup with garlic parmesan bread 41

Salad
asparagus pissladiere with grape fondue 101
Caesar 90
cress and herb with botrytis dressing 179
sweet red 97

Salmon fish cakes with hand-cut chips and malt vinegar 50

Salmon, potato pancakes with herbed crème fraiche 63

Salt-cured salmon fish cakes with hand-cut chips and malt vinegar 50

Sashimi tuna with scorched orange dressing 85

Sauce, lemon butter 120

Seared
prawn, pumpkin and spinach rotolo 128
scallops with radish and vegetable salad 111

Shaved serrano ham, grated tomato and olive oil bread 96

Sides 164

Simple lemon chicken with mint yoghurt 141

Slow cooked chicken, orzo pasta and white beans 42

Slow-cooked lamb tortelli with poached cherries and cherry toffee 144

Slow-cooked warm lamb shoulder salad 147

Smooth scrambled eggs with smoked trout 32

Snapper fillets, panfried, with lemon butter 120

Snapper puttanesca with roasted garlic aïoli 119

Soufflé
banana and citrus with rich chocolate sauce 186
hot French chocolate 185
passionfruit 190
raspberry meringue 182

Soup, truffle honey and parsnip 98

Spatchcock, lemon-spiced with cous cous 138

Spice apple with semolina pudding, apple pie spiced syrup 196

Spice roasted pumpkin with ricotta and sage nut butter prawns 131

Spinach and mushroom croustada 160

Summer beef carpaccio and caesar salad 90

Sweet pastry cases 230

Sweet red salad 97

Syrup
simple 260
sugar 260

Tapas 104

Tapenade, black olive 74

Tea-soaked prunes 221

Trout
cold-smoked with warm fennel broth 102
ocean with hiramasa kingfish and citrus dressing 69

Truffle honey and parsnip soup 98

Tuna, jamon and tomato 110

Tuna, sashimi with scorched orange dressing 85

Veal, grilled chops with risotto 159

Veal, peppered ribs with celeriac purée 154

Veal, rare with fennel involtini 72

Walnut praline 219

Watermelon and ginger oyster shots 59

Wet-cured ocean trout and hiramasa kingfish, with citrus dressing 69

Winter beef carpaccio with roasted black pepper oil and scorched onions 91